The Incredibly Indispensable

Web Shopping

Directory

CLARE DE VRIES

Published by
KOGAN PAGE
in association with

DAILY✠EXPRESS

natwest.com   LINE◌NE

Publishers' note
Every possible effort has been made to ensure that the information contained in this book is accurate at the time of going to press and neither the publishers nor the authors can accept responsibility for any errors or omissions, however caused. No responsibility for loss or damage occasioned to any person acting, or refraining from action, as a result of the material in this publication can be accepted by the editor, the publisher, Express Newspapers or the author.

First published in 2000

Kogan Page Limited   Kogan Page (US) Limited
120 Pentonville Road   163 Central Avenue, Suite 4
London N1 9JN   Dover, NH 03820, USA

Kogan Page website: www.kogan-page.co.uk

Daily Express website: www.express.co.uk

British Library Cataloguing in Publication Data

A CIP record for this book is available from the British Library.

ISBN 0 7494 3493 7

Cover design by Richard Reid
Typeset by Saxon Graphics Ltd, Derby
Printed and bound in Great Britain by Thanet Press Ltd, Margate

contents

introduction

art, antiques & collectibles · 1

auctions · 6

books & magazines · 8

bridal · 13

cars · 16

financial `45`

food & drink `48`

gifts `52`

health & beauty `57`

hobbies `61`

homes & gardens `64`

sports `96`

telephones & mobiles `103`

tickets `106`

travel `108`

contents

Shopping as you like it!

If you like shopping and hate the hassle, shopping with LineOne is the easy and fun alternative. Shopping is one of the fastest growing activities on the Internet. People are turning to online shopping for many reasons, the main ones being ease of use and convenience. There are a huge range of products to choose from, and often at lower prices than you'll find on the high street.

Peace of Mind
If you're worried about security of shopping online, LineOne - one of the UK's leading Internet Service Providers - has set up its own shopping charter to ensure an additional level of excellence in online customer service. All retailers in the Charter are carefully selected and monitored by LineOne so that you can be completely confident about buying products and services online.

Great Deals
Shopping with LineOne is easy, safe and fun. Choose from a vast array of products and you can pick up some great bargains and member offers along the way. The LineOne Travel section is also one of the best on the Internet offering a one-stop service with a broad range of travel information and special offers.

Compare prices on thousands of products with checkaprice!

Local Call Rates Apply

You'll find discounts on over a million flights, thousands of hotels, car hire and package holidays including over 150,000 late deals. And you can book online or by 'phone . So if you like the idea of online shopping and want to shop in the comfort of your own home, join LineOne today! It's so easy.

▶ Fast, reliable Internet access

▶ No subscription charges

▶ 5 email addresses

▶ controls to protect children's access

▶ 24 hour online support

▶ FREE £5 amazon.co.uk book voucher

▶ FREE Multimedia CD-ROM worth up to £29.99

Try LineOne Today!
It's so easy.

introduction

how to use this book

Online shopping is revolutionising our lives. Not only does it save time, money and stress from crowds, but it's fun and about as 21st century as you can get. First, people tentatively bought CDs and books from the net; now, more confident, we're getting the entire contents of our homes – the weekly food shop, computers, fridges, clothes, cosmetics and even cars – delivered right to our doors.

This book assumes that you are already acquainted with the Internet, know how to connect, are online and ready to shop, shop, shop. We work on a listings basis. The listings give the name and address of the websites but are not reviewed because we believe you just want to go to the sites without being bogged down by endless descriptions. If the site is included in this book in the first place, it means we like it because at the time of going to press it:

● is secure;

● downloads relatively speedily;

● delivers to the UK if based abroad;

● is easily navigable and clearly designed;

● has an interesting range of products for sale.

With a few exceptions, all the sites listed *close the deal* are ones on which you can carry out the entire buying process on the net. Once you've finished the shopping process, the goods will be on their way to you without additional phone calls or emails. Because of this, some sites that you may already be familiar with and normally use for research are *not* included.

As the sites aren't reviewed, they have been carefully categorised. Most of the chapters have a general section to begin with, which includes the sites that sell a wide selection within that category. For instance, sites in the **General** section of **Gardens** will sell plants, garden furniture and tools. After that, the subsections or specialist sites within categories are listed alphabetically. For instance, the **General** section of **Books** has sites that sell all types of books. As you go further down, however, you find specialists in areas such as **Business** and **Children** – sites that deal only in business books and books for children. This does not mean you won't find business and children's books in the **General** section, however.

If you are just having a browse, say in **Health & Beauty**, the **General** sites are a good place to start: they sell a selection of everything from make-up to body lotions or skincare products. But if you're looking for just skincare products, there is a specialist section further down.

Because we specialise in shops that close the deal, we do not list a property section. It is not possible to buy a house over the net – and a good thing too. You need to view your home and get a professional surveyor in before you consider handing over any money, so if anyone offers to complete over the Internet, avoid them like the plague.

Finally, read the contents list carefully so that you are familiar with all the categories we list and where they are placed. **Toys**, for example, are listed in **Children**, whilst **Games** (i.e. computer games) can be found under **Music, DVDs, Games & Videos.** Some categories have been repeated – for instance you will find **Telephones & Mobile Phones** in **Electronics** and **Office Supplies** as well as in a chapter of their own. However, rest assured that this *Incredibly Indispensable* guide has more than 2,000 individual shopping sites. We aim to make your shopping experience hassle-free and enjoyable.

safe shopping

The inevitable first question on anyone's lips when new to shopping on the Internet is: IS IT SAFE?

The answer is YES. In fact, it is somewhat safer than buying over the phone, as long as the site uses SSL (Secure Sockets Layer) technology. This means that any information you send over the net is encrypted so that only the intended recipient can read it. What happens is this: the web server sends a signal to your browser asking it to switch to secure mode. When the browser replies, the server sends over a certificate of authentication that is used to create a special code that will encrypt data. Anything you type in is encrypted before being sent over the Internet. It can still be accessed, but because it's in code, no-one else can read it.

To check whether a site is secure or not:

- Look for safe/secure accreditation logos such as Which?, Webtrader, IMRG and TrustUK. These are schemes that have checked the site for reliability, security, privacy and authenticity. The US accreditation logos include Truste, VeriSign, Cybertrust, Entrust, P3P and DigiSign. (However, if websites don't display these logos, it doesn't necessarily mean they're not secure).

- Look for a closed padlock or key icon in the status bar at the bottom of your browser window.

- Look for 'https://' instead of 'http://' at the beginning of the URL (Uniform Resource Locator, otherwise known as the site's address).

- Check the Help or FAQ section – this should provide security details.

As well as SSL, there is now also SET (Secure Electronic Transmission). This was developed by Visa and MasterCard as a better way to pay and is an electronic bank account as well as a secure channel.

Other tips for secure shopping are:

- Use the sites recommended in this book! They have all been checked and were secure at the time of going to press.

- Look for contact details such as an address and phone number on the site and test them.

- Pay by credit card. American Express guarantees purchases made on the Internet using their card. If you are the victim of a fraud, the chances are your credit card company will accept liability after the first £50. Just be prompt in reporting suspicious purchases. If a shop goes bust before they ship out to you, you can also claim against the credit card company.

- Use websites with good reputations.

- Do not disclose passwords or logins.

- Check out 'www.fraud.org' and 'www.scambusters.com' regularly for the latest net frauds and ensure you don't go anywhere near them.

privacy

Even when you don't register on a website, the company that runs the site knows which sections you have browsed and which web browser you use. They can gather a lot of information about you without you realising. When you buy something, you will always have to fill in your name, address, email address, phone number and credit card details, but try not to fill in any unnecessary details such as your marital status or age. If sites are too interested in small details such as this, they could be compiling information to sell on to direct marketing organisations.

In short, make sure that the site you're shopping from has a privacy policy. There is often a link in small letters at the bottom of the home page. Or look in the Help or FAQ sections. A privacy policy should state that your information will not be passed on to anyone else. You do NOT want to receive unsolicited email from other companies. If the company wants to send you information on other products they think you might be interested in, they should make this clear when you are buying or registering on the site, and offer you an opt-out clause. Read the opt-out clause carefully: sometimes you need to tick the box in order *not to* receive information, sometimes you tick in order *to* get it.

other shopping tips

- ALWAYS check the delivery/shipping costs and check if tax (VAT) is added. If you are buying from abroad you may also have to pay customs duty as the goods enter the country. These can sometimes add a scary amount onto your final price, so it's best to be aware of them.

- PRINT OUT records of your transactions and details of your purchases.

- ALWAYS check out the returns policy of a site. Many sites will allow you to return goods even if there's nothing wrong with them, but many DON'T.

consumer rights

You are protected by consumer rights laws on the Internet just as if you were buying from ordinary shops. When buying from UK Internet sites you are covered by UK law, which states that goods must be:

- of satisfactory quality;

- fit for use;

- as described on the website.

You are also protected by manufacturer's guarantees. But if you buy a product from the US, this will often not cover you in this country – definitely check before you buy, because you may be able to extend the warranty to European countries. If something goes wrong and you have to pay for repairs, you'll lose any savings you might have made.

Assuming the goods you have bought are faulty:

- Tell the retailer immediately. Any delay will be interpreted as acceptance on your part and work against you. You will need all relevant details: when you bought the goods, what they are, how much you paid, how you paid, etc.

- Accept the retailer's offer to mend the goods but do not accept them if they still don't work afterwards.

- Return the goods. You do NOT have to pay the return expenses.

- You may be offered a credit note for future purchases or a replacement, but you can insist on a full refund instead, if that's what you want.

If you just don't like the goods, you will be relying on the shop's goodwill policy. It is up to them whether they let you return the goods or not. In this case the steps to follow are the same as above, except this time you may have to pay the return expenses and you cannot insist on a full refund.

Be warned. Buying from individuals is a much riskier business than from retail outlets, because compensation for goods that don't live up to their description is very difficult to obtain. With faulty goods, if none of the above works then COMPLAIN. With a bit of luck a phone call should provide you with a refund. But if not, take matters further.

complaining

There are several companies you can complain to. If the retailer is part of an association, direct your complaints to the association, who will check their code of practice to see if their rules have been violated and take up the cause on your behalf. Some Internet associations are:

TrustUK	www.trustuk.org.uk
Which? WebTrader Scheme	www.which.net/webtrader
Interactive Media Retail Group	www.imrg.org

Next, get advice from the
   Office of Fair Trading   www.oft.gov.uk

Next, try an intermediary who will try to sort out the problem for you:

iLevel	www.ilevel.com
Internet Consumer Assistance Bureau	
	www.isitsafe.com

Next, try the Citizens Advice Bureau:

      www.nacab.org.uk

If the advertising of a product is the problem, complain to the Advertising Standards Authority (ASA): www.asa.org.uk

According to the ASA you do not have to pay for goods you no longer want – for instance if they have taken a ridiculously long time to arrive. The typical time limit for deliveries is thirty days.

If your complaint regards financial services, try the Financial Services Association: www.fsa.gov.uk

Finally try a lawyer, but be warned – taking a retailer to court is timely and costly.

If you have had a bad experience, let websites that post information about offending retailers know, so that other people don't have to go through the same experience. If a company realises such information about them is being disseminated, they may be encouraged to mend their ways. You can post information onto the following sites:

Bad, Better & Best Businesses	www.webBbox.com
BizRate	www.bizrate.com

searching

If you use a site from this book, you can rest assured that it is a secure site, that it ships overseas if it is not based in the UK (foreign sites have their country of origin in brackets after their names), that it has a good range of products and downloads relatively quickly.

However if you want to search for other shops, always use a specialist shopping directory. All the major portal sites provide shopping directories but these are not always the best.

The following sites are good for English shopping directory sites:

British Shopping Links	www.british-shopping.com
Buy.co.uk	www.buy.co.uk
IMRG Shops Directory	shops.imrg.org
iShop	www.ishop.co.uk
myTAXI	www.mytaxi.co.uk
Shops On The Net	www.shopsonthenet.com
ShopSmart	www.shopsmart.com

General-purpose search engines include:

Altavista	www.altavista.co.uk
Excite	www.excite.co.uk
Google	www.google.com
Lycos	www.lycos.com
Northern Light	www.northernlight.com
Search UK	www.searchuk.com
Yahoo!	www.yahoo.co.uk
Yell	www.yell.co.uk
UK Directory	www.ukdirectory.co.uk
UKMax	www.ukmax.com
UKOnline	www.ukonline.co.uk
UKPlus	www.ukplus.co.uk
Web Crawler	www.webcrawler.co.uk
What's Online	www.whatsonline.co.uk

hot bots

Hot Bots are price comparison websites. They can save both time and money. Type in the item you're looking for and the hot bot runs from site to site compiling a list of the e-stores that sell your item and at what price. When you've scrolled through the results and chosen your favourite, you can then click on the link which takes you straight through to the relevant page.

All of this sounds great. But keep in mind that:

- Bots do not search every shop. They search a limited range of sites only.

- Some bots are sponsored by a particular company or brand, which means that their information, as with much else on the Internet, is not completely independent. They charge companies and in return place them high up on their results listings.

- Some bots don't provide shipping or delivery info.

- Bots are best for products that are easy to compare, like books, CDs, videos, games, etc. They are not so good for 'a red lycra skirt with a slit up the side'. Their capability range is limited.

Some tips, therefore:

- Use an independent bot (although some of these *also* take money to list companies at the top of the search results).

- Be specific. Just typing in 'TVs' will get you all sorts of makes and models, which could be confusing.

- Scroll through all the results listed.

- Use more than one bot.

- Compare shipping prices. These hidden costs can often undo a good deal.

All in all hot bots are a good thing – they keep prices down as retailers know their products won't show up if priced too highly. As time goes on the technology will become more sophisticated and the bots will be able to deal with more products.

Good bots to use for the UK are:

BookBrain.co.uk	www.bookbrain.co.uk (sticks to books as its name suggests)
BT Spree	www.btspree.com
Buy.co.uk	www.buy.co.uk (for home utilities such as gas or electricity)
Computer Prices UK	www.computerprices.co.uk (for computers)
DealTime UK	www.dealtime.co.uk
HotBot	www.hotbot.com

Kelkoo.com	www.kelkoo.com
myTAXI	www.mytaxi.com
ShopSmart	www.shopsmart.com

Good hot bots for the US are:

DealTime	www.dealtime.com (deals with both US and UK books, CDs and videos)
mySimon	www.mysimon.com
RoboShopper	www.roboshopper.com
CNET Shopper	www.shopper.com
BottomDollar	www.bottomdollar.com
PriceScan	www.pricescan.com

auctions

Auctions are an entertaining way of finding bargains and unusual items on the net. Auction sites even make a profit: they charge a small amount for each item sold and are often selling thousands of items per day. There are three different types of auctions on the net:

- where individuals sell to individuals;

- where sites sell items for a retail company;

- traditional auctions that take place in real time, but where you participate via the net rather than being there or participating by phone.

Reverse auctions are also becoming popular. These are when consumers send details of what they're looking for and how much they're willing to pay for it. Examples of these are the US sites 'www.priceline.com' or 'www.respond.com'. However this guide deals with conventional auction sites.

registration

Usually you are asked to create a login name and password, supply contact details and a credit card number: remember therefore to use only auction sites using safe servers. Read the site's Terms and Conditions as regards delivery policies – if you are buying from an individual then you are probably responsible for delivery costs.

categories

Items for sale are organised in categories, just like any other retail website. Check the images very carefully –this is your only leg to stand on should you feel the item is not up to scratch later when you actually receive it. Ask any questions you like before bidding.

bidding

Log on, using your login name and password. You may be given a number for identification purposes. For the item you have chosen, you are told the time remaining, the latest bid, the starting price and whether there is a reserve or not. This is a price that has to be matched in order for the goods to be sold. You may not be told the reserve price – this is quite normal. Type in the figure you wish to bid and press the 'submit' button. Your bid will show up on screen in a few minutes.

Online auctions often take a few weeks. Rather than logging on every five minutes to see if you've been outbid, you can opt for the automated bidding facility. This means you enter the highest amount you are prepared to bid and the site's computer will bid for you until your limit has been reached. It only bids if someone else puts in a higher bid, so this doesn't mean you will necessarily go to your highest price every time. You don't have to use this system. Some sites send emails each time you have been outbid.

winning

If you win, you are contractually obliged to buy the goods. Unless you have bought from an official dealer, the site will leave the delivery of the goods up to yourself and the seller to organise. You should contact the seller and they should contact you. Organise your time and date of delivery. Pay by credit card if you can – that way you're a little protected should something go wrong. If you're spending large amounts of money, use an escrow service such as 'www.iescrow.com' or 'www.tradesafe.com', though the payment has to be made in US dollars. QXL has a SafePay system set up on 'www.qxl.co.uk'. They hold the money for you until you have received the goods and are happy with them.

placing an auction ad

This is very simple. Fill in an online application form giving details of what you want to sell. You can add a graphics file with your submission if you want to have an image attached to your ad. Check which format (JPEG, Bitmap, etc) the site prefers. If you attach an image, be sure to check the site has uploaded it correctly.

If you sell your item, you have to pay a fee to the site – usually a percentage of the final selling price. You will also have to pay a small listing fee for being included on the site.

cautionary notes

- Know what you want to spend. Don't get caught up in the competitive, 'win, win, win' aspect of auctions or you could be parting with a great deal of hard-earned cash.

- Use a reputable auction site.

- Don't do business with sellers who won't provide their name, address and phone number. If the seller has sold goods on the auction site before, they will have a rating from other buyers as to how quickly they provided information, sent the goods, etc. Check this rating out.

- Pay by credit card if you can.

- Research the goods. Find out what they normally sell for, using hotbots, so as to make sure you're getting a good deal. Find out from the seller as much as you can about the goods.

- Check out the site's guidelines on what to do if something goes wrong: some sites will reimburse a certain amount if the goods you bought aren't to your satisfaction. Others are just venues for trading and accept no responsibility whatsoever.

- Sometimes things go wrong because of the complex computers the auction sites use. Therefore, print off all important pages when bidding and when successful. If you don't like what you finally get, you can try complaining to the vendor but you are unlikely to get anywhere as your statutory rights are fewer than when buying from an ordinary retailer. Complaining to the auction website won't do much good either, but you can rate the seller poorly on the website.

- The bottom line is that auction sites work *entirely* on trust. SO, with that in mind, keep your wits about you and happy auctioneering.

buying from abroad

The beauty of the web is in its global reach. The main point of buying from abroad is the amount of money you can save. In this book we list sites from all over the world: the country of origin is in brackets after the name of the website. However, we concentrate mainly on British sites. This is because lots of foreign sites don't deliver to the UK (though those listed in this book do at time of going to press). There are other points that make the global reach of shopping on the Internet less attractive:

- The goods may take ages to arrive.

- If faulty, it will be expensive and difficult to send them back to their country of origin for repair.

- Items aren't always guaranteed in the UK.

- The goods may not always work over here, so always check specifications. For instance, videos from the US in NTSC format are unusable in the UK.

- Your statutory rights are restricted. You are less protected when buying from abroad.

- Shipping, import duty and VAT can sometimes eliminate your savings, as can varying exchange rates. The amount you calculated at the time of buying may be different from when the money is actually debited from your card. The rules on duty and VAT are complicated (and seemingly random). So check the rate you'll need to pay at 'www.hmce.gov.uk/general/question/index.htm' or call 020 7202 4227. Then multiply that rate by the price and add the result to the price. Then add VAT, usually 17.5%. You do not need to do this for items valued at less than £18; £36 if they're gifts.

If things go wrong when buying from abroad, contact the Citizens Advice Bureau ('www.nacab.org.uk') or the Office of Fair Trading ('www.oft.gov.uk') for assistance.

spam emails

Many new email programmes have filtering devices to prevent time-wasting and inbox-clogging emails coming through. (These are known as spam emails.)

As most direct marketing companies are members of the Direct Marketing Association (DMA), registering your email address on the email preference list with the DMA will ensure that you are unsolicited by the majority of these companies. Click on the email preference service link on 'www.dma.org.uk' or go to 'www.e-mps.org/en'.

If you do receive spam email, be sure not to reply. Eventually you will be dropped from the list.

The Internet Watch Foundation (IWF) is supported by the Department of Trade & Industry. It is an independent body that deals with harmful material on the Internet such as child pornography. They are contactable 24 hours a day: by phone on 08456 00 88 44, by email at report@internetwatch.org.uk and on their website: 'www.iwf.org.uk'.

Data Protection Registrar   www.dpr.gov.uk/index.html

Office of Fair Trading   www.oft.gov.uk/html/shopping

Trading Standards Office   www.tradingstandards.gov.uk

art, antiques & collectibles

Although you're unlikely to buy a Rembrandt over the net, there is plenty of art with which to decorate your home. Equally there are many sites for collectibles and antiques. Don't forget the auction sites, which also have a plethora of art, antiques and collectibles to bid for.

antiques
art
collectibles

antiques

Antique Collectibles	www.antique-collectables.com
Eureka I Found It!	www.eureka-i-found-it.com
Gentry Antiques	www.gentryantiques.co.uk

art

general

Acquired Images Gallery (US)	www.artlink.net
Ancient & Oriental	www.antiquities.co.uk
Art-Afrika	www.art-afrika.com
Art Areas (US)	www.artareas.com
Art & Parcel	www.artandparcel.com
Art.com (US)	www.art.com
Art Is A Tart	www.art-is-a-tart.com
Art Net (US)	www.artnet.com
Art Open (Australia)	www.s-central.com.au/artopen
Art Selection (Thailand)	www.art-selection.com
Art Store	www.design-uk.com/art_store
Atelier Walter Ehrismann (Switzerland)	www.ehrismann.com
Chinese Gallery	www.thechinesegallery.co.uk
Chorley & Saunders Golf Fine Art	www.golf-print.com
Craig Campbell Golf Art	englishhall.com/cc/cc/cchome.html

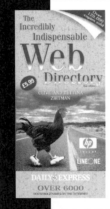

Earth Gallery	www.earthgallery.net
Gallery On The Net	www.galleryonthenet.co.uk
Gallery Wired	www.gallerywired.com
Heaton Cooper Studio	www.heatoncooper.co.uk
Ireland Exposed	www.irelandexposed.com
Keens Secure Art Galleries	www.keen-art.com
LS Lowry.com (US)	www.lslowry.com
Masai Mara	www.masai.u-net.com
Nature Art Network (US)	www.nature-art.net
Peter Reading's Online Art Gallery	www.peter-reading.co.uk
Podd Limited	www.podd.co.uk
Portraits of Britain Online	www.portraitsofbritain.co.uk
Sally Mitchell Fine Arts	www.sallymitchell.com
Scottish Art	scottish-art.com
Shorelines Gallery — Sailing Pictures	www.shorelines.co.uk
Students' Gallery	ws.safestreet.co.uk/StudentsGallery
Zoë Art.com	www.zoeart.com

prints & posters

Artland	www.artland.co.uk
Art Republic	www.artrepublic.com
Art Worldwide	www.art-worldwide.com
Easyart Prints & Posters	www.easyart.com
Francis Frith Classic Prints	catalogue.barclaycard.co.uk/ cgi-bin/frith.storefront
GB Posters	www.gbposters.com
Irish Poster Company	www.theirishpostercompany.com
P4Posters	www.p4posters.com
Poster Gallery (US)	www.postergallery.com
Poster Shop	www.postershop.co.uk
Push Posters	www.pushposters.co.uk
Scottish Print Shop	www.scottish-prints.co.uk
Titanic Prints	www.titanicprints.com
Vintage Magazine Co	www.vinmag.com
World Gallery	www.worldgallery.co.uk

collectibles

general

Abbey Records — Vinyl Records	www.abbeyrecords.com
Bears At The Real McCoy	www.ulsterpages.com/realmccoy2
British Museum Company	www.britishmuseum.co.uk
Clarice Cliff Collectors' Store	www.claricecliff.com/shopping
Collectibles Online	henleyhighstreet.inetc.net/ col/acatalog
Corgi Shop	www.corgi-shop.co.uk
Cowtraders	gotogifts.co.uk/for/cows
Creative Foto Concepts (US)	www.creativefotoconcepts.com
Crown Devon Musicals Online	www.crowndevon.com

Dollies Bear Gère	www.dolliesbear-gere.com
DSC Showcases & Display Cases	dscshowcases.co.uk
eFilmposters	www.efilmposters.com
Eggceptional Africa	www.eggceptional.co.za
Essentially English	www.essentially-english.com
Griffin Collectibles	www.griffin-collectables.co.uk
Khan Handcrafted Stone Sculptures	www.khanimports.com
Maryon Victoriana	www.victoriana.co.uk
Mulberry Bush	www.mulberrybush.com
Native Son Designs (US) — Native American Collectibles	www.powerplace.com/atpost/dunn
Owl Barn	www.the-owl-barn.com
Pewter Collectibles	www.pewter.co.uk
Piggin	www.piggin.com
Recollections — Rock Music Memorabilia	www.recollections.co.uk
Sewill's Clocks, Weather & Nautical Instruments	www.sewills.com
Shrubbery Direct Dolls	www.dolls-direct.co.uk
Someone Special (US)	www.someonespecial.com
Stamporium — Rubber Stamps	www.stamporium.f9.co.uk
The Teapottery	gotogifts.co.uk/for/teapots
Titanic Incorporated	www.titanic-inc.com
Vindolanda Roman Collectibles	www.vindolanda.com
When We Were Young	www.whenwewereyoung.co.uk
Whittontique	www.whittontique.co.uk

celebrities

Alfie's Celebrities' Autographs	www.alfies.com
Artstars — Celebrity Portraits	www.artstars.co.uk
Total Autographs	www.totalautographs.co.uk

china & ceramics

Commex International Ltd — Ceramics & China	www.tableware.org.uk
Isis Decora Porcelain Designs	www.gotogifts.co.uk/for/porcelain
Lladro Porcelain	lladrogib.hypermart.net/llindex.html

crafts

Allegria Arts & Crafts	www.allegria.co.uk
Countrycrafts	www.countrycrafts.co.uk
Crafts Antiques Online (US)	www.craftsantiques.com
Craftfolk	www.craftfolkww.com
Russian Crafts	www.russian-dolls.co.uk

figurines

Ballantynes Of Walkerburn Figurines	www.ballantynes-walkerburn.com
Distant Realms Figurines	www.greenroomstudio.co.uk

maps

Border Art — Ancestral Maps   www.borderart.com
Richard Nicholson Of Chester —
   Antique Maps & Prints   www.antiquemaps.com

military

All Things Military   www.allthingsmilitary.co.uk
Battle Orders Ltd — Arms &
   Armour   www.battleorders.co.uk

miniatures

Chantry Miniatures   www.curiosity-shops.co.uk/chantry
Malyns Miniatures   www.malyns.com

models

4 Mil Models Toy Soldiers   www.4milmodels.com
Bagnalls Car Models   www.bagnallsmodels.co.uk
Goldone Selection Model Boats   www.goldone.co.uk
JP Editions Model Castles   www.collectorsgallery.com/jp/
   index.html
Model Cars   www.model-cars.co.uk
Racing Models   www.racing-models.com

stamps

Abstamps   www.abstamps.co.uk
Just Wendy Themes   stamps.estreet.co.uk/stamps
National Wildlife Philatelics (US)   www.nationalwildlife.com

art, antiques & collectibles

5

auctions

See the sections on auctions in the **Introduction** for a full guide to how auctions work.

QXL   www.qxl.com
Net auctions are a completely trust-reliant environment and this site has made the shopping process as safe as possible with features like the escrow service.

Amazon (UK)	www.amazon.co.uk
Amazon (US)	www.amazon.com
Antiques World (Belgium)	www.antiques-world.com
Aucland	www.aucland.com
The Auction Channel	www.theauctionchannel.co.uk
Auction Connect	www.auctionconnect.lycos.com
Auction Town	www.auctiontown.co.uk
Auction Universe	www.auctionuniverse.co.uk
Auction Zone UK	auctionzone.co.uk
Bezign — Fashion & Lifestyle	www.bezign.com
Bid.com (Ireland)	www.bid.com
Bid Find (US)	www.vsn.net
Blue Cycle	www.bluecycle.com
Bonham's	www.bonhams.com
CQOut Online Auctions	www.cqout.com
Deal Deal (US) — Computers & Electronics	www.dealdeal.com
eBay (UK)	www.ebay.co.uk
eBay (US)	www.ebay.com
eBid UK Online Auctions	www.ebid.co.uk
Fired Up	www.firedup.com
First Auction (US)	www.firstauction.com
Gavelnet.com	www.gavelnet.com
Goricardo	www.goricardo.co.uk
iCollector	www.icollector.com
Internet Auction List (US)	www.internetauctionlist.com
ITSeller — Computer Auctions	www.itseller.com
Last Minute	www.lastminute.com
London Art — Art Auctions	www.londonart.co.uk/auction
Lot 1 Auctions	www.lot1.com
Phillips	www.phillips-auctions.com/uk
Popula	www.popula.com
Pottery Auction	www.potteryauction.com
QXL	www.qxl.com
Sotheby's	www.sothebys.com
Sporting Auction	www.sportingauction.com
UTrade Auctions	www.utrade.com
What Am I Bid? Auctions	www.whatamibid.com
Wine Bid	www.winebid.com

auctions

books & magazines

Online book retailers were one of the first web success stories – and now there are thousands of bookshops out there, including many specialists.

books
magazines

books

general

AA Bargain Books	www.aabargainbooks.co.uk
Abooks	www.a-books.com/system/shopassistant.htm
Amazon (France)	www.amazon.fr
Amazon (UK)	www.amazon.co.uk
Apple Bookshop	www.applebookshop.co.uk
Bags Of Time	www.bagsoftime.com
Barnes & Noble	www.barnesandnoble.com
Blackwell's	bookshop.blackwell.co.uk
Bloomsbury	www.bloomsbury.com
BOL	www.uk.bol.com
Bookstore	www.bookstore.co.uk
BookCloseOuts	www.bookcloseouts.com
The Book People	www.thebookpeople.co.uk
The Book Place	www.thebookplace.com
Booksamillion	www.booksamillion.com
BookZone	www.bookzone.co.uk
Border's	www.borders.com
Cambridge University Press	uk.cambridge.org
Country Bookshop	www.countrybookstore.co.uk
The Daily Express Bookshop	www.bcvd.net/express
Dorling Kindersley	www.dkonlinestore.co.uk
Escape	www.escapefiction.co.uk
Gilliham's	www.gillihams.co.uk
Heffer's	www.heffers.co.uk
Kogan Page	www.kogan-page.co.uk
Long Barn Books	www.longbarnbooks.co.uk
Manx	www.manxbooks.com
My Bookshop	www.mybookshop.com
Osborne Books	www.osbornebooks.co.uk
Penguin	www.penguin.co.uk
Quality Paperbacks Direct	www.qpd.co.uk
Red Onion Books	www.redonionbooks.com
Saxon's	www.saxons.co.uk
Scotbooks	www.scotbooks.com
Streets Online	www.alphabetstreet.infront.co.uk
Student Book World	www.studentbookworld.com
Toby Press	www.tobypress.com
Waterstone's	www.waterstones.co.uk
WH Smith	www.whsmith.co.uk
Wordsworth	www.wordsworth.com

academic

Sage Publications	www.sagepub.co.uk
Western Academic & Specialist Press	www.waspress.co.uk
T&T Clark Publishers	www.tandtclark.co.uk

antiquarian

Bibliofind	www.bibliofind.com
Booklovers	www.booklovers.co.uk
Collectable Books	www.collectablebooks.co.uk
Legend Books	www.legendbooks.com/legend

archaeological

Heritage Archaeological Books	www.heritageweb.com/system/index.html
Oxbow Books	www.oxbowbooks.com

art

The Arts' Guild	www.artsguild.co.uk

aviation

Airlife Publishing	www.airlifebooks.com/system/shopassistant.htm

business

The Economist	www.bookshop.economist.com
Kogan Page	www.kogan-page.co.uk
McGraw-Hill Bookstore	www.bookstore.mcgraw-hill.com

children

Children's Book Centre	www.childrensbookcentre.co.uk
Discovery	www.discoverybookclub.co.uk
Funorama	www.funorama.co.uk
Lion Publishing	www.lion-publishing.co.uk

computers

Computer Step	www.ineasysteps.com

conspiracy

Conspiracy	www.4rie.com

cookery

Cookerybooks.com	www.cookerybooks.com

dance

Dancebooks.co.uk	www.dancebooks.co.uk

dolls' houses

Mulberry Bush	www.mulberrybush.co.uk

educational

Schofield & Sims	www.schofieldandsims.co.uk

books

engineering
American Technical Publishers   www.ameritech.co.uk

environmental
Earthscan   www.earthscan.co.uk

food
Taste   www.tasteonline.co.uk

ireland
Eason   www.eason.ie
Read's Irish Bookstore   www.readireland.ie

maps
Map Source Inc   www.mapsource.com

maritime
Bookharbour.com   www.kh-online.co.uk

medical
STM   www.stmbooks.co.uk

motoring
Motorail   motorail.e-webshopping.co.uk/
front.html

music
Sanctuary   www.sanctuarypublishing.com/shop

pets
Pet Bookshop   www.petbookshop.com

science fiction
Fantasy & Science Fiction Club   www.fsf.co.uk

sport
Sports Books   www.sportsbooksdirect.co.uk
Sportspages   wwww.sportspages.co.uk

talking books
Internet Talking Bookshop   www.goodreading.co.uk/audio/
main.html

technical
Top Floor Publishing   www.topfloor.com

theatre
Internet Theatre Bookshop   www.stageplays.co.uk

books

travel

Escape Travel   www.travelbookclub.co.uk

magazines

1st Choice Magazines   www.1stchoicemagazines.cjb.net
British Magazines   britishmagazines.com
Magazine Shop   www.magazineshop.co.uk

bridal

Your wedding is too important for you to want to buy a dress over the web without trying it on first. The wedding websites, therefore, sell gifts, rings and honeymoons, but advertise dresses rather than sell them. The US is ahead of the UK in terms of good wedding sites. This is why we suggest them for research, although unfortunately they often only deliver domestically.

Confetti   www.confetti.co.uk
From budget planners to details on how to marry abroad, this site covers everything. There is a good search facility of suppliers in your area. Stylish gifts too.

general
balloons
bridalwear
catering
champagne
fireworks
flowers
gifts
honeymoons
insurance
lists
rings
stationery

general

The US sites are included for research purposes only, as they do not deliver to the UK.

Confetti	www.confetti.co.uk
Divine Weddings (US)	www.divineweddings.com
The Knot (US)	www.theknot.com
Web Wedding	www.webwedding.co.uk
Wedding Channel (US)	www.weddingchannel.com

balloons

Balloon Box UK	www.zednet.co.uk/balloonboxuk
Balloon People	www.balloonpeople.net
Balloon Saloon	www.balloongreetings.co.uk

bridalwear
dress ideas

Alternative Gowns	www.alt-gowns.com
Basia Zarzycka	www.basia-zarzycka.co.uk/gowns.htm
Bridal House	www.bridalhouse.co.uk
Brides Direct	www.bridesdirect.co.uk/pages/ bridalcat.html
Cloud Nine	www.cloudninebridal.co.uk
Confetti	www.confetti.co.uk

Excellent site, with rotating dresses for better browsing.

Divine Weddings (US)	www.divineweddings.com
The Knot (US)	www.theknot.com
Pronuptia	www.pronuptia.co.uk
Web Wedding	www.webwedding.co.uk
Wedding Channel (US)	www.weddingchannel.com

garters

Elizabeth Cooke	www.nottingham-lace.co.uk

tiaras

Celtic Bride	www.celticbride.com
Tiaras by T	website.lineone.net/~tiara
Ursula Wildy Tiaras	www.ursulawildy.co.uk

veils

Pauline Nichol	www.bridalveils.co.uk

catering

Fantasia Caterers	www.fantasia-caterers.com

champagne

★ Don't forget *Wine* in *Food & Drink* too.

Champers Direct	www.champersdirect.co.uk

fireworks

Finesse Fireworks   gotogifts.co.uk/for/fireworks

flowers

★ Don't forget *Flowers* in *Gifts* too.

Chantal Florist   www.chantalflorist.co.uk
Floral Touch   www.floraltouch.co.uk/weddings.htm
Flower Works   www.actionflowers.com
Netflora   www.netflora.co.uk

gifts

★ Don't forget our entire chapter on *Gifts*.

Postagift   www.postagift.com
Web Wedding   www.webwedding.co.uk

honeymoons

★ Don't forget to visit *Travel*.

Web Wedding   www.webwedding.co.uk

insurance

Alder Broker   www.abgltd.co.uk/wedding_
                                      insurance.htm

lists

Debenham's   www.debenhams.co.uk

rings

Jewels   www.jewels.co.uk
John Park Jeweller   www.johnpark.co.uk

stationery

Debenham's   www.debenhams.co.uk
Wedding Stationery   www.weddingstationery.co.uk

cars

Although there are plenty of online spare parts sites, not many car sites allow you to close the deal online. This is why this chapter is not as large as you might expect. For that reason sites which allow you to order a car are included, although the actual paying may have to be completed offline.

When buying a car online, check for hidden extras: delivery charges, government first registration fees, AA assistance, manufacturer/dealer warranties and specification fees if the car is imported from abroad.

Virgin Cars   www.virgincars.com
Because everything is included in the final price, Virgin Cars is our favourite car site. There is also a futuristic-sounding 'design your own car' feature and substantial savings to be made.

general
accessories
audio
car phones
registration
roofing systems

The following sites help you research the car you want, although you cannot actually order or buy online. When you have chosen a car you're interested in, you enter your details (over a secure connection) and the dealers then contact you.

autobytel.co.uk	wwwautobytel.co.uk
Auto Trader	www.autotrader.co.uk
Carseekers	www.carseekers.co.uk
Carsource	www.carsource.co.uk
Classic Car.com	www.classicar.com
Classic Motor Monthly	www.classicmotor.co.uk
Exchange & Mart	www.ixm.co.uk/motor
What Car?	www.whatcar.co.uk

general

Drive The Deal	www.drivethedeal.com
Jamjar	www.jamjar.com
Virgin Cars	www.virgincars.com
One Swoop	www.oneswoop.com

   Allows you to order your car, though the transaction is not completed online.

accessories

Autosave	www.autosave-scotland.co.uk
Edworthy's Auto Electrics	www.edworthys.co.uk
North Eastern Land Rover	www.nelandrover.co.uk

audio

Audio In Car	www.malltraders.com/audioincar
Blue Spot Car Audio	www.bluespot.co.uk
Car Audio Direct	www.caraudiodirect.com
In Car Express	www.incarexpress.co.uk

car phones

Interzone Communications	www.wireless-telecom.co.uk/system/index.htm

registration

Emark	www.emark.co.uk

roofing systems

Hartwell Shop	www.hartwell-shop.co.uk

cars

children

The net is particularly useful for exhausted parents who can get nappies, food and many other items delivered to the door without having to worry about getting the kids to the supermarket, unpacking the buggy, lugging the family around the shop and then carrying everything back.

JoJo Maman Bebé   www.jojomamanbebe.co.uk
Adorable children's clothes. Stylish and practical maternity wear.

babies
christenings
clothes
toys
travel accessories

babies

All About Parents	www.allaboutparents.com
Active Birth Centre	www.activebirthcentre.com
Babies 'R' Us	www.babiesrus.co.uk
Baby Best Buy (US)	www.babybestbuy.com
Babycare Direct	www.babycare-direct.co.uk
Baby City	www.babycity.co.uk
Babycrest	www.babycrest.com
Baby Directory	www.babydirectory.com
Baby Gem	www.babygem.com
Babyworld	www.babyworld.co.uk
Boots — Mother & Baby Section	www.boots.co.uk
Daisy Diapers	www.daisydiapers.com
The Great Little Trading Company	www.gltc.co.uk
Interstitch — Baby Quilts	www.interstitch.co.uk
Kiddicare	www.kiddicare.com
Little Duck — Prams & Pushchairs	www.littleduck.co.uk
Mothercare	www.mothercare.com
NY Style (US)	www.nystyle.com
Over The Moon Babywear	www.overthemoon-babywear.co.uk
Rudra UK	www.rudrauk.com
The Total Baby Shop	www.thetotalbabyshop.com
Twinkle Twinkle — Eco-Friendly Nappies	www.twinkleontheweb.co.uk
Urchin	www.urchin.co.uk
Wahh!	www.wahh.net

christenings

Christening UK	www.christening.uk.com
Kiddijoy Christening Shoes	www.baby-shoes.co.uk
Personal Presents	www.personalpresents.co.uk

clothes
children

★ Don't forget the baby sites listed above that stock baby clothes.

Boomerskids (US)	www.boomerskids.com
Childrenswear	www.childrenswear.co.uk
Cotton Moon	www.cottonmoon.co.uk
Jo Jo Maman Bebé	www.jojomamanbebe.co.uk
Kids' Stuff	www.kids-stuff.co.uk
Mothercare	www.mothercare.com
One Of A Kind Kid (US)	www.oneofakindkid.com
Poppy Childrenswear	www.poppy-children.co.uk
Schoolwear Centre	www.schoolwear-centre.co.uk
Tots & Teens	www.totsandteens.co.uk
Tots 2 Teens	www.tots2teens.com

children

maternity

Blooming Marvellous	www.bloomingmarvellous.co.uk
Bumps Maternity Wear	www.bumpsmaternity.com
Dorothy Perkins	www.dorothyperkins.co.uk
JoJo Maman Bebé	www.jojomamanbebe.co.uk
Long Tall Sally	www.longtallsally.com
Mothercare	www.mothercare.com
Next	www.next.co.uk
NY Style (US)	www.nystyle.com
One Hot Mama	www.onehotmama.com

toys

★ Don't forget *Teddy Bears* in *Gifts*.

general

Barbie	www.barbie.com
Beanie Pets UK	www.beaniepets.com
Bear World	www.bearworld.co.uk
Character Warehouse	www.character-warehouse.com
Dawson & Son	www.dawson-and-son.com
Dolly Crafts	www.dollycrafts.co.uk
Early Learning Centre	www.elc.co.uk
eToys	www.etoys.co.uk
FAO Schwartz (US)	www.fao.com
Funstore	www.funstore.co.uk
Genius Babies (US)	www.geniusbabies.com
Grannie Annie's Beanie Store	www.grannie-annie.co.uk
Hamley's	www.hamleys.co.uk
Huggables Teddy Bears	www.huggables.com
Internet Gift Store	www.internetgiftstore.co.uk
Klikit — Scale Model Kits	www.klikit.co.uk
Krucial Kids — For 0-8 Year Olds	www.krucialkids.com
Little Wonder Toys — For 0-7 Year Olds	www.littlewonders.co.uk
Mail Order Express	www.mailorderexpress.co.uk
Peter Rabbit & Friends Gift Shop	www.lakefield-marketing.co.uk
Pokémon	www.pokemon.uk.com
Puzzles & Toys.com	www.webstreet.co.uk/11
Sindy	www.sindy.com
Toy Chest	www.toychest.co.uk
Toys 'R' Us	www.toysrus.co.uk
Toy Town	www.toytown.co.uk
Toy UK	www.toy.co.uk
Toy World Store	www.toyworldstore.com
Toy Zone	www.toyzone.co.uk
Very Important Little People	www.viponline.co.uk

children

board games

Apollo Board Games	www.toysave.co.uk
Chess Shop	www.chess-shop.co.uk
Dominoes	www.dominoes-highstreet.co.uk
The Games Shop	www.gameshops.co.uk
Games Web	www.games-web.co.uk
Just Jigsaws	www.justjigsaws.com
London Bridge Centre	www.bridgemagazine.co.uk
London Chess Centre	www.chess.co.uk
Masters' Traditional Games	www.mastersgames.com
Puzzle Plus	www.puzzleplus.com
The Sports Game Shop	www.sportsgameshop.com
TC's Jigsaw Puzzles	www.jigsaw-puzzles.co.uk
Wentworth Wooden Jigsaw Puzzles	www.wooden-jigsaws.com

travel accessories

Family on Board (US)	www.familyonboard.com

cigars

Fine Cubans, Dominicans and Nicaraguans can be bought on the net. If you buy from one of the many US sites, be sure that your customs duty is included in the final price.

Aardvark Cigars   www.aardvarkstore.com
Aardvark stocks over 300 rolled cigars, plenty of accessories and a good seven-cigar sampler pack.

Aardvark Cigar Club	www.aardvarkstore.com
AE Lloyd	www.aelloyd.com
Cambridge Wine	www.cambridgewine.com/ cigarintro.html
Cigar Export (US)	www.cigarexport.com
Cigars 4 You (US)	www.cigars4u.com
Cigs Online (US)	www.cigsonline.com
Corona Cigar (US)	www.coronacigar.com
James Barber Tobacconist	www.smoke.co.uk
JJ Fox	www.jjfox.co.uk
Maxibond	www.cubans.co.uk
Pipe Shop (US)	www.pipeshop.com

clothes

The amount of successful clothing retail sites is partly due to the catalogue mail order business, which meant that many of the sites already had the infrastructure to deal with large orders.

Topshop www.tops.co.uk
For fabulously-priced, high street styles, Topshop can't be beaten. They even have sales on the net. Very fast downloading. It's the best.

general
accessories
hats
hip/latest trends
jeans
kilts
knitwear
leather jackets
men
outdoor gear
shirts
shoes
socks
swimwear
ties
T shirts
vintage
waistcoats
women

general

These sites include a combination of clothes, shoes and accessories for men and women.

Abercrombie & Fitch	www.abercrombie.com
APC (France)	www.apc.fr
AW Rust	www.awrust.co.uk
BargainNet	www.bargainnet.co.uk
Best Of British	www.thebestofbritish.com
Bluefly (US)	www.bluefly.com
Boden	www.boden.co.uk
Branded Stocks	www.brandedstocks.co.uk
Brooks Brothers (US)	www.brooksbrothers.com
Clothing Connection	www.clothingconnection.co.uk
Debenham's	www.debenhams.co.uk
Esprit	www.esprit-intl.com
Fashion Net (US)	www.shop.fashion.net
Fashion Outlet	www.fashion-outlet.com
Freeman's	www.freemans.com
Gossypium — The Eco Cotton Store	www.gossypium.co.uk
Grass Roots	www.g-roots.com
Gremino	www.gremino.com
Hawkshead	www.hawkshead.com
House Of Bruar	www.houseofbruar.com
Into Fashion	www.intofashion.com
Kay's	www.kaysnet.com
Land's End	www.landsend.co.uk
La Redoute	www.redoute.co.uk
London Wide	www.londonwide.co.uk
Metropolis	www.metropolis-clothing.com
Net Sale	www.netsale.co.uk
Next Directory	www.next.co.uk
QVC	www.qvcuk.com
Racing Green	www.racinggreen.co.uk
Studio Moda (Italy)	www.studiomoda.com
Ted Baker	www.swerve.co.uk
Zercon	www.zercon.com
Zoom	www.zoom.co.uk

accessories
general

Accessorize	www.accessorize.co.uk
Celtic Sheepskin	www.celtic-sheepskin.co.uk

hosiery

Clothes Line	www.the-clothes-line.co.uk
Divina Windsor	www.divinawindsor.co.uk
Legs Express	www.legsexpress.com

| Silk Stockings | www.silk-stockings.co.uk |

jewellery & watches

Abooga	www.abooga.com
Approved Diamonds	www.approveddiamonds.com
Celtic Watches	www.celtic-watches.com
City Clocks	www.cityclocks.co.uk
Direct Watch Company Ltd	www.directwatch.com
Ermani Bulatti	gotogifts.co.uk/for/bronze
eTreasures	www.e-treasures.co.uk
Fashion Crazy	www.fashioncrazy.net
Finecraft Jewellery	www.finecraftjewellery.com
Fortunoff	www.fortunoff.com
Gold Jewellery	www.gold-jewelry.co.uk
Goldscene Jewellery	www.goldscene.co.uk
Great British Jewels	www.gbj.co.uk
Half Price Jewellers	www.hpj.co.uk
Ice Cool	www.icecool.co.uk
Internet Jewellery & Gemstones	www.ijag.com
Jewellers' Net	www.jewellers.net
Jewellery Unlimited	www.jewelleryunlimited.com
Jewels	www.jewels.co.uk
Pearl-e	www.pearl-e.co.uk
Silver Plus Gold	www.silverplusgold.co.uk
Scottish Jewellery	www.scottish-jewellery.co.uk
Studio Jupiter	www.studio-jupiter.com
Sovereign Diamonds	www.sovereigndiamonds.com
Traser Watches	www.traser-uk.com
Watch Factory (US)	www.watchfactory.com
Watch Heaven	www.watch-heaven.com

scarves

Heritage Cashmere Pashminas	www.heritage-cashmere.co.uk
Nepal	www.webstreet.co.uk/nepal

sunglasses

Anglo-American Eyewear	www.angloamericaneyewear.com
Bowman Edge	www.bowman-edge.co.uk
Dollond & Aitchison	www.danda.co.uk
Eyeglasses (US)	www.eyeglasses.com
Retrospecs	www.retrospecs.co.uk
Spexonline	www.spexonline.net
Vision3k.com	www.vision3k.com

hats

The Cap Factory	www.thecapfactory.co.uk
James Lock Hatters	www.lockhatters.co.uk

hip/latest trends

Sites for both men and women.

2 Ways	www.2ways.co.uk
Brown's Focus	www.brownsfashion.com
Clothes Store	www.theclothesstore.com
Cyberdog	www.cyberdog.co.uk
Diesel	www.diesel.co.uk
Fat Face	www.fatface.co.uk
Surf On The Net	www.surfonthenet.co.uk
Underground (Germany)	www.underground-fashion.de

jeans

Madhouse	www.madhouse.co.uk

kilts

Classic Kilts	www.classickilts.com
House of Scotland	www.house-of-scotland.com
Kilts Online	www.highland-dress.co.uk

knitwear

Bill Baber	www.billbaber.com
Christian Scott	www.christianscott.com
Cyber Sweaters (US)	www.cybersweaters.com
Guernsey Knitwear	www.guernseyknitwear.co.uk
Carraig Donn Irish Knitwear	www.carraigdonn.com

leather jackets

Anne Dreske-Somoff Leather	www.aaaaustralia.com.au/ somoffhp.html

men

4XL — Long Trousers For Long Legs	www.forxl.co.uk
Atlas Kingsize — For Very Large Sizes	atlas-menswear.com
Brandshop — Leisure Wear	www.brandshop.co.uk
Bugle Boy	www.bugleboy.com
Burton Menswear	www.burtonmenswear.co.uk
Clothing Trends — Designer Bargains	www.clothingtrends.co.uk
Designer Heaven	www.designerheaven.co.uk
Designer Online	www.designeronline.co.uk
Dressmart	www.dressmart.co.uk
Eastwood Clothing	www.eastwoodclothing.com
Hugestore	www.hugestore.com
Joe Brown's	www.joebrowns.co.uk
Morija	www.morija.com
Ozwald Boateng	www.ozwald-boateng.co.uk

Peter Werth	www.peterwerth.co.uk/clothes1.html
Rubens Menswear	www.rubensmenswear.com
SAVIshopper	www.savishopper.com
Swerve	www.swerve.co.uk
Top Man	www.topman.co.uk
UK Designer Shop	www.ukdesignershop.com
Wolsey Menswear	www.eshopone.co.uk/home_wolsey.html

outdoor gear

Big Day	www.bigday.co.uk
Born For Loden	www.born-for-loden.co.uk
Carry On Clothing	www.carryonclothing.co.uk
Outdoor Supplies	www.outdoorsupplies.co.uk
Rohan Adventure Clothing	www.rohan.co.uk
Wild Day	www.wildday.com

shirts

men & women

| Pink | www.thomaspink.co.uk |
| Shirtsearch | www.shirtsearch.co.uk |

men

Café Coton	www.cafecoton.co.uk
Cavenagh Shirts	www.cavenagh.co.uk
Charles Tyrwhitt	www.ctshirts.co.uk
Joseph Turner Shirts	www.josephturner.co.uk
Pink	www.thomaspink.co.uk
Shirt Press	www.shirt-press.co.uk

shoes

men & women

Barratt's	www.barratts.co.uk
Clifford James	www.clifford-james.co.uk
Jones Bootmaker	www.jonesbootmaker.com
Ozzy's Discount Footwear	www.ozzys.co.uk
Regalos Country & Western Store — Cowboy Boots	www.linedancing.co.uk
Safety Footwear Shop	www.idml.co.uk
Shopeeze	www.shopeeze.com
Softmoc (US)	www.softmoc.com
Shipton & Heneage	www.shiphen.com
Shoedini (US)	www.shoedini.com
Shoes Direct	www.shoesdirect.co.uk
Shoe Shop	shoe-shop.com
Sports Shoes	www.sportsshoes.co.uk

men only

clothes

Bexley (France)	www.bexley.com
Big Men Big Feet	www.largemen.co.uk
Big Shoes	www.bigshoes.com
Crockers Of Hungerford	www.classicshoes.co.uk
Ducker & Son	www.duckerandson.co.uk
Eastwood Clothing	www.eastwoodclothing.com
Marcus Shoes	www.marcusshoes.com
Pediwear	www.pediwear.co.uk
Tim Little	www.timlittle.com

socks

The Clothes Line	www.the-clothes-line.co.uk

swimwear

Action Fit	www.actionfit.com
Beach Queen	www.beachqueen.com
Ujena	ujena.co.uk

ties

Fox & Chave	www.foxandchave.co.uk
Sumina Silk Ties	www.sumina.co.uk
Tie Rack	www.tierack.co.uk
Tieshop	www.tieshop.uk.com

t shirts

Amego	www.amego.co.uk
Novelty Togs	www.noveltytogs.com
T Shirt King (US)	www.t-shirtking.com
T Shirt Shop	www.tshirtshop.co.uk

vintage

Andrew Wurst Vintage Clothing	www.awgm.com/vintage/catalog.htm

waistcoats

Lois Gaunt	www.webstreet.co.uk/loisgaunt

women

Sites often include a selection of shoes and accessories.

2001	www.2001wear.co.uk
April Cornell (US)	www.aprilcornell.com
Artigiano – Italian Fashion	www.artigiano.com
Alight – Sizes 14-26 (US)	www.alight.com
Black Frock	www.blackfrock.com
David Nieper Designer Clothing	www.eshopone.co.uk/ home_david.html
Dorothy Perkins	www.dorothyperkins.co.uk
eArmoire	www.earmoire.com
Also has accessories.	

clothes

Elsa Haag	www.elsahaag.co.uk
Evans	www.evans.ltd.uk
Fassy Fashions	www.fassyfashions.com
Kingshill	www.kingshilldirect.com
Long Tall Sally	www.longtallsally.com
Luly K (US)	www.lulyk.com
Monsoon	www.monsoon.co.uk
Penny Plain	www.pennyplain.co.uk
Principles	www.principles.co.uk
Red Herring	redherringshoes.com
Topshop	www.tops.co.uk

clothes

computers

The substantial savings to be made on computers from the States means that buying computerware on the net is very popular. You can even build your own computer on many of the sites. However, warranties rarely extend outside the US. If you're prepared to be responsible for all repairs, you could get yourself a bargain. Consult the section on **Buying From Abroad** in the **Introduction** before buying. If you're looking for games, you'll find them in **Music, DVDs, Games & Videos**.

Software is one of the best things to buy on the Internet. You save shipping charges, money and time by downloading the product directly to your computer once you have paid for it. Your computer will give you a choice as to whether you save the software onto disk or directly onto your computer's hard drive.

Download time is shortened by most files being compressed before they get onto the Internet. Any file ending in EXE (for PCs) or SEA (for Macs) will decompress itself automatically. Zip files (for PCs) or SIT (for Macs) will need an unzip programme. You probably already have one installed on your machine; if not, get one from 'www.winzip.com'. Downloading usually involves your web browser talking to an FTP server, which is a computer that stores files. Sometimes the FTP server may be protected, in which case you have to logon and create a password.

Blue Circuit Ltd www.bluecircuit.com
Quick to download, easily navigable, great range of products, good savings.

general
hardware
software

general

21 Store	www.21store.com
Action Computer Supplies	www.action.com
Adaptec	www.adaptec-europe.com
Andrew Scott	www.andrew-scott.co.uk
Apple Store	www.store.apple.com
Big Save	www.bigsave.com
Blue Circuit Ltd	www.bluecircuit.com
Buy.com	www.buy.com
Capital Technology	www.capital.uk.com
Clarashop	www.clarashop.com
Clove Technology	www.clove-tech.co.uk
Comet	www.comet.co.uk
Comm Store	www.commstore.co.uk
Compaq	www.compaq.co.uk
Computer Shopper (US)	www.computershopper.com
Computer Warehouse Online	www.cwonline.co.uk
Custard Computers	www.custard-computers.co.uk
Dabs Direct	www.dabs.com
Damson	www.sbs-sales.co.uk/damson
Dell UK	www.dell.co.uk
Dixon's	www.dixons.co.uk
Egghead (US)	www.egghead.com
Elonex	www.elonex.co.uk
Eurosystems	www.eurosystems.co.uk
Evesham Micros	www.evesham.com
Gateway 2000	www.gw2k.co.uk
Global Direct	www.globaldirect.co.uk
Hewlett Packard	www.hpstore.hp.co.uk
IBM	www.pc.ibm.com/uk/buydirect
Index	www.indexshop.com
Insight	www.insight.com
Jungle	www.jungle.com
Just PC	www.just-pc.net
LineOne	www.lineone.net

LineOne
www.lineone.net

Maxx PC	www.maxxpc.com
MISCO Computer Products	www.misco.co.uk
Morgan Computers	www.morgancomputers.co.uk
Novatech	www.novatech.co.uk
Office Online	www.office-online.co.uk
Outpost (US)	www.outpost.com
PC World	www.pcw-software.co.uk/shop

computers

CLAIM YOUR
FREE GIFTS
WORTH UP TO £34·99

Rollcage (Ref: CO10)

ClickArt 10,000 (Ref: CO11)

Family Tree (Ref: CO06)

Oxford Encyclopedia (Ref: CO12)

DO3D (Ref: CO02)

All you want from the Internet

✓ Fast reliable Internet access

✓ No subscription charges

✓ Exclusive member discounts

✓ 5 email addresses

✓ 50MB web space

✓ Controls to protect children's access

✓ 24-hour online customer support

To join LineOne and claim your free gift call
0800 111 210
or join online
www.lineone.net

LINE●ONE

Local call rates apply.

Preston Computers	www.prestoncomputers.co.uk
QXL	www.qxl.com
Special Reserve	www.reserve.co.uk
Simply Computers	www.simply.co.uk
Technomatic	www.technomatic.co.uk
Technoworld	www.technoworld.co.uk
Tempo	www.tempo.co.uk
Tiny	www.tiny.com
Totally Portable	www.totallyportable.com
UK Computing	www.ukcomputing.com
Vector Online	www.vectorpc.co.uk
Viglen	www.viglen.co.uk
Watford	www.watford.co.uk
WStore	www.wstore.co.uk

hardware

Adata	www.adata.co.uk
AJP	www.ajp.co.uk
CHL Office Supplies	www.offserv.co.uk
Compu b Apple Store (Ireland)	www.compub.net
Dan	www.dan.co.uk
Hi Grade	www.higrade.com
Image Computer Systems (Australia)	www.s-central.com.au/ imagecomputers
Jaycee's Computer Shop	www.jaycees.co.uk
Laptop Shop	www.laptop-shop.co.uk
Mesh	www.meshplc.co.uk
PC Index — A Hotbot For Computer Hardware	www.pcindex.co.uk
Pico	www.picosystems.co.uk
Prosser's Online	www.prossers.co.uk
Protégé Systems	www.protege-systems.co.uk
T2K Technology 2000	www.t2k-technology2000.co.uk
TCX Computers	www.tecnix.co.uk
Telemart Systems	www.telemart.co.uk
Teltec	www.teltec.co.uk
Ultra Violet	www.ultra-violet.com

batteries

GMK Batteries	www.gmkbatteries.co.uk
MDS Batteries	www.mdsbattery.co.uk

cables

Euronet Computer Cables	www.euronetwork.co.uk
Lightwave Cables	www.computer-cables.com

components

Dan Peripherals	www.dpltd.co.uk
Displays Online Components	www.review-displays.co.uk

Browse

Buy

...opping has never been easier, especially if ...u're thinking of buying equipment for the home ...home office.

...st take a look at what's on sale at the HP Home & ...me Office Store. You'll find everything - from ...ernet-ready PCs that also play DVDs, photo-quality ...lour printers, fast, high-quality scanners to superb

All-in-Ones that not only print, they scan, copy and fax as well, and even CD burners for recording your own music. And not forgetting the latest megapixel digital cameras, perfect for taking pictures to send to friends and family electronically!

Browse for as long as you like - and then buy at the HP Home & Home Office Store.

...isit www.hp.com/uk/buy.html or call 0870 606 4747

Net Shop	www.netshop.co.uk
Redstore PC Components	www.redstore.com
RS Components	rswww.com
Stem Online Shop	www.stemsys.co.uk
Techdirect Components	www.techdirect.net
TSI Europe	www.tsi-europe.com

ink & cartridges for printers

Aah-Haa Inkjet Supplies	www.aah-haa.com
Ink & Stuff	www.inkandstuff.co.uk
The Ink Factory	www.theinkfactory.co.uk
Inkjet 4 U Office Supplies	www.inkjet4u.co.uk
Integrex	www.integrex.co.uk
Printer Supplies	www.printersupplies.co.uk

memory

Crucial Technology	www.crucial.com/uk
Memory Store	www.memorystore.co.uk
Offtek	www.offtek.co.uk

monitors

Kingmaker Flat Panels	www.kingmaker.co.uk
Taxan	www.taxan.co.uk
Trident Online	www.tridentonline.com

mp3s

Digital Dream	www.digitaldreamco.com
Jaz Piper	www.mediaforte.nl/jazpiper/en_ie/index.htm
MP3 Players	www.mp3players.co.uk
Worldwide Innovations	www.innovate-world.com

software

Amazon	www.amazon.co.uk/software
Beyond (US)	www.beyond.com
CD House	www.cdhouse.co.uk
CD Imports	www.cdimports.com
CD-R Media	www.cd-rmedia.co.uk
Chumbo	www.chumbo.co.uk
Computermate	www.compmate.com
Demo Room (US)	www.demoroom.com
Distributor Systems	www.dsiweb.co.uk
Dolphin Computer Music	www.dolphinmusic.co.uk
Download	www.download.com
Easyworks	www.easyworks.co.uk
Electronics Boutique	www.eb.uk.com
Eon Solutions Shareware	www.eon-solutions.com
Futuretail	www.futuretail.com
Gaelsoft	www.gaelsoft.com

Global Voice	www.globalvoicelimited.com
GSP Software	www.gspltd.co.uk/Shop.asp
Guildsoft Ltd	www.guildsoft.co.uk
Intuit — Quick Financial Software	www.intuit.co.uk
ItSoft	www.itsoftmedia.com/en
Learning Store	www.learningstore.co.uk
The Lobby	www.thelobby.co.uk
Microworld	www.microworld.co.uk
Open Soft	www.opensoft.co.uk
PC Home	www.pchome-eshop.co.uk
Power Quest	www.powerquest.com
The Project Shop	www.webstreet.co.uk/theproject
QBS Software	www.qbss.com
Red Leaf	www.redleaf.co.uk
Soft By Net	www.softbynet.com
Software That Scores — For Football Lovers	bt.icat.com/store/ alternative-software
Software Pages	www.softwarepages.co.uk
Software Paradise	www.softwareparadise.co.uk
Software Partners	www.softpart.co.uk
Software Savings	www.softwaresavings.co.uk
Timebomb Y2K Software	www.time-bomb.co.uk
Widget Software	www.widget.co.uk

educational

Berlitz	www.berlitz.com
Born 2 Learn	www.born2learn.com
Linguaphone	www.linguaphone.co.uk
Proops	www.proops.com
Talkfast	www.talkfast.com

department stores

Visit Bloomingdales without the seven-hour plane ride first! For other large stores, don't forget the chapter on **Malls**. Note that the US department stores do deliver to the UK but may only take orders by phone or fax.

The Best of British www.thebestofbritish.com
The design is so elegant and clean it's impossible not to be drawn in. Their children's section has a good mix ranging from clothes to toys to babies' needs.

Argos	www.argos.co.uk
Barclay Square	www.barclaysquare.co.uk
Bentall's	www.bentalls.co.uk
The Best Of British	www.thebestofbritish.com
Bloomingdales (US)	www.bloomingdales.com
Brands For Less	www.brandsforless.com
Buckingham Gate	www.buckinghamgate.com
Cameron Square	www.cameronsquare.com
Debenham's	www.debenhams.co.uk
EDirectory	www.edirectory.co.uk
EshopOne	www.eshopone.co.uk
eWebC3	www.ewebc3.com
Global Power	www.globalpower.co.uk/next.html
Go Bazaar	www.gobazaar.co.uk
Harrods	www.harrods.co.uk
John Lewis	www.johnlewis.com
Kay's	www.kaysnet.com
Let's Buy It	www.letsbuyit.com
Macy's (US)	www.macys.com
Neiman Marcus (US)	www.neimanmarcus.com
New York First (US)	www.newyorkfirst.com
Presents Direct	presentsdirect.com
QVC UK	www.qvcuk.com
Shop!	www.shop-i.co.uk
Shopping Thai	shoppingthai.com
Shops Direct	www.shopsdirect.co.uk
Woolworth's	www.woolworths.co.uk

electronics

Fridges, freezers, washing machines, cameras, hi-fis —
every electronic need is catered for on the web. Great
discounts are available, so search diligently.

★ Don't forget the *Department Stores,* many of which also have electrical sections.

general

Sites selling TVs, hifis, cameras, dishwashers, etc.

Appliance Direct	www.appliance-direct.co.uk
Argos	www.argos.co.uk
AV Store — Sony	www.av-store.co.uk
Bargains UK	www.bargains.uk.com
Be Direct	www.bedirect.co.uk
Bes Direct	www.bes-direct.co.uk
Best Buy Home Appliances	www.best-buy-appliances.co.uk
Best Stuff	www.beststuff.co.uk
Beyond HiFi	www.beyondhifi.com
Big Save	www.bigsave.com
Buy Electrical Direct	www.bedirect.co.uk
Clara Shop	www.clarashop.com
Comet	www.comet.co.uk
Digital Choice	www.digitalchoice.co.uk
Dixon's Online	www.dixons.co.uk/shops
Electrical Appliances Direct	www.electricalappliancesdirect.co.uk
Electrical Discount UK	www.electricaldiscountuk.co.uk
Electrical Warehouse	www.electricalwarehouse.co.uk
Empire Direct	www.electricalsdirect.co.uk
Go Digital	www.godigital.co.uk
Hutchison's	www.hutchisons.co.uk
Index	www.indexshop.com
Intersaver	www.intersaver.co.uk
Let's Buy It	www.letsbuyit.com
Marketplace 4 U	www.marketplace4u.com
Miller Brothers	www.millerbros.co.uk
One Stop Electronics (US)	www.vstore.com/vstoreelectronics/world
Price Hero	www.pricehero.co.uk
Quality Electrical Direct	www.qed-uk.com
QVC	www.qvcuk.com
QXL	www.qxl.com
Rings Electrical	www.ringselectrical.com
Sharp Electronics	www.sharp.co.uk
Shop!	www.shop-i.co.uk
Techtronics	www.techtronics.com
Tempo Electrical	www.tempo.co.uk
Top Electrical	www.topelectrical.co.uk
Trident Online Technology Store	www.tridentonline.com
Unbeatable	www.unbeatable.co.uk
Value Direct	www.value-direct.co.uk
Virtual Electrical	v-e.usp.net/virtual-electrical/home.cfm
Web Electricals	www.webelectricals.co.uk
ZDNet	www.zdnet.com

electronics

cameras & camcorders

1st Cameras Online	www.1stcameras.co.uk
21 Store	www.21store.com
All Cures	www.allphotoshop.com
Battery Home	www.batteryhome.com
Cameras Direct	www.camerasdirect.co.uk
Canon	www.canon.co.uk
Digital Camera Company	www.digital-cameras.com
Digital Depot	www.digitaldepot.co.uk
Digital Dream	www.digitaldreamco.com
Euro Foto	www.euro-foto.com
Fujifilm (US)	www.fujifilm.com
Henry's CCTV Centre	www.cctv-centre.co.uk
Internet Cameras Direct	www.internetcamerasdirect.co.uk
Jack's Camera Shop	www.jackscamera.com
Jessops	www.jessops.com
Kamera Direct	www.kamera-photo.co.uk
KEH (US)	www.keh.com
Kenmore Camera	www.kcamera.com
Lyons' Stop 'n' Shop	www.lyonsstopnshop.com
Mailshots Film	www.mailshots.co.uk
Mustek	www.mustek.com
Photo Forum	www.photoforum.co.uk
Photographic Direct	www.photographicdirect.co.uk
Picstop	www.picstop.co.uk
Rush Online – Digital Imaging	www.rush-on-line.co.uk
Sherwood's Photo	www.sherwoods-photo.com
Tek Discount Warehouse (US)	www.tekgallery.com
UK Digital	www.ukdigital.co.uk

dvds

Bargains UK	www.bargains.uk.com
Code Free DVD	www.codefreedvd.com
DVD Guys (US)	www.dvd-guys.com
DVD World	www.dvdworld.co.uk
Mail UK	www.mailuk.com
Techtronics	www.techtronics.com
UK DVD	www.ukdvd.com

hi-fis

Audio Atmosphere	www.audioatmosphere.com
Exchange Shop	www.exchangeshop.co.uk
Flatspeakers	www.flatspeakers.net
HiFi Bitz	www.hifibitz.co.uk
Online Hifi Store	catalogue.barclaycard.co.uk/ cgi-bin/audio.storefront
Purley Radio	www.purleyradio.co.uk
Richer Sounds	www.richersounds.com
Sapphire's Sound & Light	www.mixers.co.uk

electronics

home appliances

2001 Appliances	catalogue.barclaycard.co.uk/cgi-bin/d2001.storefront
Appliance Direct	www.kitchen-appliance.co.uk
Appliance Online	www.applianceonline.co.uk
Cookers Online	www.cookersonline.com
Freenet Electrical Appliances	www.freenet.ltd.uk
Home Electrical Direct	www.hed.co.uk
Household Appliances Direct	www.householdappliancesdirect.co.uk
Net Appliance	www.netappliance.co.uk
Trade Appliances	www.trade-appliances.co.uk
UK Appliance	www.ukappliance.co.uk
White Box	www.whitebox.co.uk
Woodall's Electrical	www.we-sell-it.co.uk/elec.html

telephones & mobile phones

4 Phones	www.4phones.co.uk
AC Communications	www.accomms.com
Bargain Phones	bargain-phones.co.uk
Beyond 2000	www.beyond2000.uk.com
BT Shop	www.btshop.bt.com
Budget Phone	www.budgetphone.co.uk
Buy A Mobile Phone	www.buyamobilephone.co.uk
Carphone Warehouse	www.carphonewarehouse.com
Cellnet	www.cellnet.co.uk
Dial A Phone	www.dialaphone.co.uk
ETC Communications	www.etccomms.co.uk
Freedom Phones	www.freedomphones.co.uk
Free Mobile Phones	www.freemobilephones.net
Ifone	www.ifone.co.uk
JM Communications	www.jmcomms.net
Miah Telecom	www.miahtelecom.co.uk
Mobile Bargains Store	www.mobilebargains.com
Mobile Now	www.mobilenow.co.uk
Mobile Phone Network	www.mobilephone-net.com
Mobile Phones Online	www.talkcentre.co.uk
The Mobile Republic	www.themobilerepublic.com
MobileShop	www.mobileshop.com
Mobiles UK	www.mobilesuk.net
One2One	www.one2one.co.uk
One Shop For All	www.oneshopforall.com/uk/mobilephone_shop.html
Orange	www.orange.net
Orange People	www.orangepeople.co.uk
Orange Phones	www.orange-phones.co.uk
The Pay As You Go Mobile Phone Store	payasyougo.bizland.com
Phone Shop	www.phoneshop.uk.com
Phone Factory	www.phonefactory.com

Phone Warehouse	www.phonewarehouse.co.uk
Small Talk Communications	www.prepays.co.uk
Storm Mobiles	www.storm-online.com/mobile
Student Mobiles	www.studentmobiles.com
Talking Shop	www.talkingshop.co.uk
Talk Mobiles	www.talkmobiles.co.uk
Telephones Online	www.telephones-online.co.uk
Tiger Mart	www.tigermart.co.uk
Time 2 Talk Communications	www.time2talk.co.uk
Totally Portable	www.totallyportable.com
UK Phone Shop	www.ukphoneshop.com
Vodafone Retail	www.vodafone-retail.co.uk

mobile accessories

Accessories 4 U	www.accessories4u.co.uk
Axex	www.axex.co.uk
Beyond 2000	www.beyond-2000.co.uk
Mobile Facias	www.mobilefacias.co.uk
Mobile Rings — Nokia Only	www.mobilerings.co.uk
Mobile Tones — Nokia Only	www.mobiletones.com
Ringtones	www.ringtones.co.uk

televisions

AV Shop Direct	www.avshopdirect.co.uk
Box Clever	www.box-clever.com
Remote Controls	www.remotecontrols.co.uk
What Video & TV	catalogue.barclaycard.co.uk/ cgi-bin/tv.storefront

vacuum cleaners

Express Cleaning Supplies	www.express-cleaning-supplies.co.uk
Oreck	www.oreck.co.uk
UK Vacs	www.ukvacs.com
Vacuum Cleaners Direct	www.vacuumcleanersdirect.co.uk

video recorders & accessories

Blank Tapes	www.blankshop.com
Lektropacks	www.lektropacks.co.uk
Mediavision	www.a-v.co.uk

electronics

financial

You can save money, apply for a mortgage, trade shares and buy insurance online. There are now also several online banks. Security is clearly an issue for any online financial business and most of the sites are at pains to put the customers' minds at rest.

The majority of financial websites offer a lot more advice than online products. Where products such as pensions are concerned it is best to discuss your needs with a financial advisor before closing any deals.

general
advice
banks & building societies
credit cards
insurance
investments
mortgages
share dealing

general

Pensions, loans, mortgages, insurance, savings etc.

Equitable Life	www.equitable.co.uk
Prudential	www.pru.co.uk
Scottish Widows	www.scottishwidows.co.uk
Standard Life	www.standardlife.co.uk
Woolwich	www.woolwich.co.uk

advice

American Stock Exchange	www.amex.com
Blay's	www.blays.co.uk
Find	www.find.co.uk
FT Quicken	www.ftyourmoney.com
Money Extra	www.moneyextra.com
Moneygator	www.moneygator.com
Money Net	www.moneynet.co.uk
Money Web	www.moneyweb.co.uk
The Motley Fool	www.fool.co.uk
Scotland Online	www.business.scotland.net
This Is Money	www.thisismoney.com
Virgin Direct	www.virgin-direct.co.uk
Wise Buy	www.wisebuy.co.uk

banks & building societies

Abbey National	www.abbeynational.co.uk
Barclays	www.barclays.co.uk
Bradford & Bingley	www.bradford-bingley.co.uk
Bristol & West	www.bristol-west.co.uk
Citibank	www.citibank.com/uk
Co-operative Bank	www.co-operativebank.co.uk
EBS Building Society	www.ebs.ie/home.asp
Egg	www.egg.com
First Direct	www.firstdirect.com
First-e	www.first-e.com/uk
Halifax	www.halifax-online.co.uk
Lloyds TSB	www.lloydstsb.co.uk
Nationwide	www.nationwide.co.uk
NatWest	www.natwest.com

Royal Bank Of Scotland	www.rbos.co.uk
Scottish Life International	www.investorsdirect.co.uk
Smile	www.smile.co.uk

credit cards

American Express	www.americanexpress.com
Barclaycard	www.barclaycard.co.uk
Mastercard	www.mastercard.com
Visa (US)	www.visa.com

insurance

Automobile Association	www.theaa.co.uk
Coversure Insurance Group	www.coversure.co.uk
Direct Line	www.directline.com
Eagle Star Direct	www.eaglestardirect.co.uk
Easycover	www.easycover.com
First Insurance Shopper	www.insuranceshopper.co.uk
First Quote Insurance	www.1stquote.co.uk
Inspop	www.inspop.com
Insurance Discounts Online	www.theidol.com
Insurance Wide	www.insurancewide.com
Jackson's Insurance Services	www.jacksonsinsure.co.uk
Norwich Union	www.norwich-union.co.uk
Screen Trade	www.screentrade.co.uk

investments

National Savings	www.nationalsavings.co.uk
NetISA	www.netisa.co.uk

mortgages

Charcol Online	www.charcol.co.uk
Fred Finds	www.fredfindsmortgages.com
The Mortgage Shop	www.mortgage-shop.co.uk
Northern Rock	www.nrock.co.uk

share dealing
information

The Wrong Price	www.thewrongprice.com

trading

Etrade	www.etrade.co.uk
Schwab Worldwide	www.schwab-worldwide.com
Standard Bank London	www.sbl.co.uk
Stock Trade	www.stocktrade.co.uk

food & drink

Every type of food imaginable is available on the web, and buying your weekly shop online is no longer a laughable idea for the future. The web is also good for small independent food shops, whose produce can now be widely disseminated. Organic produce is also very popular on the web.

Lobster.co.uk   www.lobster.co.uk
This site sells a lot more than just lobster – and all their products are luxury foods. Complete self indulgence.

Berry Bros & Rudd   www.bbr.co.uk
Excellent range of fine wines from Britain's most established wine merchant. Fascinating information and articles on wine, including charts on when to drink and when to keep your bottles. Allows you to search for wines by food, matching region or vintage.

food
drink

food

★ Don't forget there's also a section on *Hampers* in *Gifts*.

general

Best of British	www.thebestofbritish.com/shop/delicatessen
British Cornershop	www.britishcornershop.co.uk
Cakes Direct	www.thin-end.co.uk
County Foods	www.countyfoods.com
Direct Foods	www.directfoods.uk.com
Dominos — Pizza Online	www.dominos.co.uk
Ducker's	www.duckersfoods.co.uk
The Fish Society	www.thefishsociety.co.uk
Flavored Oils (US)	www.sottovoce.com
Flying Noodle	www.flyingnoodle.com
Food & Drink	www.foodndrink.co.uk
Food Ferry Company	www.foodferry.co.uk
Harpers & Son	www.harpersfood.co.uk
Heinz Direct	www.heinz-direct.co.uk
Julian Graves OnLine Shopping	www.juliangraves.co.uk
Norbury's	www.norburys.co.uk
Pepperama — Pepper Sauces	www.pepperama.co.uk
Purity Foods (US)	www.purityfoods.com

Sells Spelt, a wheat substitute for those with wheat allergies.

Room Service	www.roomservice.co.uk
Sainsbury's	www.sainsburystoyou.co.uk
Simply Simpson's	www.simplysimpsons.co.uk
St George's Square	www.stgeorgessquare.com
Tesco	www.tescodirect.com
UK Goods (US)	www.ukgoods.com

For English food lovers in the US.

Vegnet	www.vegnet.co.uk
Waitrose	www.waitrose.com
Warren Farm Shop	www.warrenfarmshop.co.uk
World Foods	www.worldfoods.co.uk

bakery

Botham	www.botham.co.uk
Fitzbillies	www.fitzbillies.com
The Village Bakery	www.village-bakery.com

cheese

Butler's Farmhouse Cheeses	www.butlerscheeses.co.uk
The Fine Cheese Company	www.finecheese.co.uk
Huge Cheese Direct	www.hugecheese.co.uk
Teddington Cheese OnLine	www.teddingtoncheese.co.uk

gourmet

The Foodstore	www.thefoodstore.co.uk
Good Food Direct	www.goodfooddirect.co.uk

Gourmet World	www.gourmet-world.co.uk
Leaping Salmon	www.leapingsalmon.co.uk
Le Gourmet Francais Online	www.gourmet2000.co.uk
Lobster.co.uk	www.lobster.co.uk
Mackenzie Ltd (US)	www.mackenzieltd.com
Morel	www.morel.co.uk

international

AG Ferrari Foods (US) — Fine Italian Foods	www.agferrari.com
Australia Shop	www.australiashop.co.uk
Brits Abroad	www.britsabroad.co.uk
Chilli Willie's Spices By Post	www.curryhouse.co.uk/cw
The Curry Sauce Company	www.currysauce.com
Ethnic Foods	www.ethnic-foods.com
Foodshop Sweden	www.foodshopsweden.m.se
Irish Express (US)	www.irish-food.com
Just Thai Chili (Singapore)	www.thaichili.com
Mount Fuji International — Japanese	www.mountfuji.co.uk/acatalog
Olivetum (Italy)	www.olivetum.com
Shopitaly	www.shopitaly.co.uk
Take It From Here — Italian Food	www.tifh.co.uk
Tamarind Fine Foods — Indian Food	www.tamarindfinefoods.co.uk
Wapishana Caribbean Gourmet	www.carib.freeservers.com

meat

Edwards of Conwy	www.edwardsofconwy.co.uk
Meat Direct	www.meatdirect.co.uk
Sweet Ithon Lamb — Welsh Lamb	www.lambdirect.co.uk
Welsh Lamb Direct	www.welshlambdirect.co.uk

organic

Fresh Food Company	www.freshfood.co.uk
Greenacres Organic Company	www.greenacresorganic.co.uk
Organic Delivery Company	www.organicdelivery.co.uk
Organics Direct	www.organicsdirect.co.uk
Roney's High Class Butcher	www.eshopone.co.uk/ home_roneys.html
Simply Organic	www.simplyorganic.net
Somerset Levels Organics	www.somersetorganics.com

smoked foods

Bleiker's Smoke House Ltd	www.bleikers.co.uk
Dundonnell Smoked Salmon	www.smokedsalmon.uk.com
Gourmets' Choice	www.gourmetschoice.net
Rannoch Smokery	www.rannochsmokery.co.uk
Riverside Smoked Foods	www.riverside-smoked-foods.co.uk

sweets

★ Don't forget *Chocolates* in *Gifts*.

Chambers' Candy	www.chamberscandy.co.uk
ChocExpress	www.chocexpress.com
Chocolate Store	www.chocolatestore.com
Cybercandy	www.cybercandy.co.uk
D&D Snacks	www.ddsnacks.co.uk
Devon Fudge Direct	www.webstreet.co.uk/devonfudge
Dr Chocolate	www.drchocolate.co.uk
Hudson Gray	www.chocolates-online.co.uk
Roger's Chocolates (Canada)	www.rogerschocolates.com
Thornton's	www.thorntons.co.uk

drink

alcoholic

Beers Direct	www.beersdirect.com
Black Bottle	www.blackbottle.com
Black Forest	www.blackforest.co.uk
Drinks Direct	www.drinks-direct.co.uk
The Drink Shop	www.thedrinkshop.com
eAbsinthe	www.eabsinthe.com
Glenturret	www.glenturret.com
Real Ale Guide	www.alestore.co.uk
Scotch Whisky	www.scotchwhisky.com
Whisky Shop	www.whiskyshop.com

wine

Amivin	www.amivin.com
Berry Bros & Rudd	www.bbr.co.uk
Bordeaux Direct	www.bordeauxdirect.co.uk
A Case Of Wine	www.acaseofwine.co.uk
Champers Direct	www.champersdirect.co.uk
Chateau OnLine	www.chateauonline.co.uk
Chelsea Bubble — Champagne	www.chelseabubble.co.uk
Fine & Rare Wines	www.frw.co.uk
It's Wine	www.itswine.com
Mad About Wine	www.madaboutwine.com
Now 365	www.now365.com
Wine	www.wine.com
Wine Cellar	www.winecellar.co.uk
Wine Online	www.wineonline.co.uk
Young's	www.youngs.co.uk/winedirect

non-alcoholic

Cappuccino Connection (US)	www.cappuccino-connection.com
Costa Rica Coffee Co	www.costaricacoffee.co.uk
E-Java Gourmet Coffee	store.yahoo.com/e-javacom
Gray & Seddon	www.gray-seddon-tea.com
Keith's	www.keiths.co.uk
Ten Ren's Tea & Ginseng (US)	www.tenren.com
Strathmore Coffee	www.we-sell-coffee.com
Whittard Of Chelsea	www.whittard.com

food & drink

gifts

Where presents are concerned, any of the sites in this book could be eligible for this category. The web has made birthday and Christmas shopping much less stressful than ever before – you can be reminded of upcoming birthdays, have your gifts wrapped and your cards sent for you. However, there have been horror stories about gifts not arriving in time for Christmas. The only thing you can do is try to leave plenty of time for ordering and check delivery schedules so as not to disappoint your loved ones.

Buyagift   www.buyagift.co.uk
Fancy a spin in a supersonic military jet fighter plane to the tune of £7,900? Or just a bouquet of flowers for £22? An amazing range of gifts in a colourful, easily navigable site.

general
balloons
cards
chocolates & sweets
flowers
hampers
jewellery & watches
men's gifts
teddy bears
unusual

★ Don't forget *Tickets*.

general

All Wrapped Up	www.allwrappedup.co.uk
Basket Case (US)	www.basket-case.com
Birthdays	www.birthdays.co.uk
Buyagift	www.buyagift.co.uk
Designer Gifts	www.designergifts.co.uk
Dial A Basket	www.heartphelt.co.uk
Emporium	www.emporiumuk.com
Fizzynet	www.malltraders.com/fizzynet
Fortnum & Mason	www.fortnumandmason.com
The Gift Delivery Company	www.giftdeliveryco.com
Gift Inspiration	www.giftinspiration.com
The Gift Service	www.giftservice.co.uk
Gifts From Scotland	www.giftsfromscotland.com
Givit	www.givit.com
Global Gifts	www.globalgifts.co.uk
House Of Ireland Gifts	store.houseofireland.com
Initial Ideas	www.initialideas.co.uk
J&M Giftware	www.jandmgiftware.co.uk
Jomono Gift Vouchers	www.jomono.com
Last Minute	www.lastminute.com
Needapresent	www.needapresent.co.uk
NickNaks	www.nicknaks.co.uk
Nik Nak Paddy Wak	www.niknakpaddywak.com
Obsessions	www.obsessions.co.uk
Out of Afrika	www.outofafrika.co.uk
Past Times Online	www.pasttimes.com
The Pied Piper Shop	www.thepiedpipershop.sagesite.co.uk
Postagift	www.postagift.com
Red Ribbon Gifts	www.redribbongifts.co.uk
SF Cody's Emporium	www.codys.co.uk
Strathclyde — Gifts From Scotland	www.scottishgifts.com
Voucher Express	www.voucherexpress.co.uk
Wheesh	www.wheesh.com

balloons

Balloon People	www.balloonpeople.net
Balloon Saloon	www.balloongreetings.co.uk
Postal Balloon	www.postalballoons.com

cards

Card Box	www.card-box.co.uk
Card Mart	www.snapcards.co.uk
Ceramic Cards	www.ceramiccards.co.uk
Clinton Cards	www.clintoncards.co.uk
Cyber Cards	www.cybercards.co.uk
Excalibur Cards	www.blacksword.currantbun.com/excaliburcards.html

gifts

Happy Birthday To You! — Singing Birthday Cards	www.happybirthdaytoyou.com
Hypersnail	www.hypersnail.co.uk
Occasions Observed	www.ocob.co.uk
Shadi Cards — For Pakistani & Indian Weddings	www.shadicards.com
Snailgram (US)	www.snailgram.com

chocolates & sweets

Browne's Chocolates	www.brownes.co.uk
Burnt Sugar Sweet Co	www.burntsugar.co.uk
Carrie-Jane's Fudge	www.carrie-janes.co.uk
Chambers Candy Company	www.chamberscandy.co.uk
Chocolate Store	www.chocolatestore.com
Cook's of Swanton	www.cooksofswanton.com
House Of Chocolate	www.thehouseofchocolate.com
Sayitwith	www.sayitwith.co.uk/chocs.html
Sugar Boy	www.sugarboy.co.uk
Sweet Seductions	www.sweet-seductions.co.uk

flowers

0800-Blossoms Ltd	www.0800-blossoms.com
Chantal Florist	www.chantalflorist.co.uk
Clare Florist	www.clareflorist.com
Expressions Flowers & Balloons	www.expressions.co.uk
Fiorito	www.fiorito.co.uk
Flower.co.uk	www.flower.co.uk
Floral Creations	www.floralcreations.co.uk
Flowers2send	www.flowers2send.com
Flower Service	www.flowerservice.co.uk
The Gift Service	www.giftservice.co.uk
Interflora	www.interflora.co.uk
London Flower Net	www.london-flowernet.com
Netflora	www.netflora.co.uk
Rainbow Flowers	gotogifts.co.uk/for/flowers
Teleflorist	www.teleflorist.co.uk
Village Greenery Florist (US)	www.thevillagegreenery.com
Sayitwith.co.uk	www.sayitwith.co.uk

hampers

800 Hampers	www.800hampers.com
Bewleys Hampers	www.bewleys-hampers.ie/contact.asp
Clearwater Hampers	www.hamper.com
Fax Fruit	www.faxfruit.com
Fortnum & Mason	www.fortnumandmason.com
French Hampers	www.frenchhampers.co.uk
Hampers Online	www.hampers-online.com

gifts

Highland Fayre — Christmas Hampers	www.christmashamper.com
Lewis & Cooper	www.lewis-and-cooper.co.uk
Virginia Hayward	www.virginia-hayward.co.uk

jewellery & watches

Abooga	www.abooga.com
Approved Diamonds	www.approveddiamonds.com
Celtic Watches	www.celtic-watches.com
City Clocks	www.cityclocks.co.uk
Direct Watch Company Ltd	www.directwatch.com
Ermani Bulatti	gotogifts.co.uk/for/bronze
eTreasures	www.e-treasures.co.uk
Fashion Crazy	www.fashioncrazy.net
Finecraft Jewellery	www.finecraftjewellery.com
Fortunoff	www.fortunoff.com
Gold Jewellery Online	www.gold-jewelry.co.uk
Goldscene Jewellery	www.goldscene.co.uk
Great British Jewels	www.gbj.co.uk
Half Price Jewellers	www.hpj.co.uk
Ice Cool	www.icecool.co.uk
Internet Jewellery & Gemstones	www.ijag.com
Jewellers' Net	www.jewellers.net
Jewellery Unlimited	www.jewelleryunlimited.com
Jewels	www.jewels.co.uk
Pearl-e	www.pearl-e.co.uk
Silver Plus Gold	www.silverplusgold.co.uk
Scottish Jewellery	www.scottish-jewellery.co.uk
Studio Jupiter	www.studio-jupiter.com
Sovereign Diamonds	www.sovereigndiamonds.com
Traser Watches	www.traser-uk.com
Watch Heaven	www.watch-heaven.com
Watch Factory (US)	www.watchfactory.com

men's gifts

Boys' Stuff	www.boysstuff.co.uk
Firebox	www.firebox.com
Gadget Shop	www.gadgetshop.co.uk
Gizmo	www.gizmoandwidget.com
I Want One Of Those	www.iwantoneofthose.com
Tamlin & Brown	www.tamlinandbrown.com
The Gentleman's Shop	www.gentlemans-shop.co.uk
Urban Man	www.urbanman.com

teddy bears

Company Of Bears	www.company-of-bears.com
Cuddlies Direct	www.cuddliesdirect.co.uk
Huggables	www.huggables.com
Hugs & Cuddles	www.hugsandcuddles.co.uk

gifts

Interteddy	www.interteddy.com
Teddy Bear Island (US)	www.bearisland.com
Teddy Express	www.teddyexpress.co.uk

unusual

Alternative Gifts	www.alt-gifts.com
Amazing Days (Ireland)	www.amazingdays.com
Autographs For Sale	www.autographsforsale.com
The Cover Company — Computer Covers	www.thecovercompany.com
Crystal Cavern	www.crystalcavern.com
Eggcentric — Ostrich Egg Clocks	www.gotogifts.co.uk/for/eggs
Essentially English Gifts	www.essentially-english.com
Firebox	www.firebox.com
Fridge Door Magnets	www.fridgedoor.com
Funky Metals	www.funkymetals.com
Gadgets Galore	gadgets-galore.hypermart.net
Get Mapping	www1.getmapping.com
Gifthouse	www.gifthouse.co.uk
Gizmo	www.gizmoandwidget.com
Grannie Used To Have One	www.grannieusedto.co.uk
Gumps (US)	www.gumps.com
Howels of Sheffield Thermometers	www.howels.com
Innovations	www.innovations.co.uk
Jones Shop (Australia) — For People Named Jones…	www.jones.com.au
Le Val D'Or — Food From The Continent	www.levaldor.com
Living Designs	www.livingdesigns.co.uk
Maps Worldwide	www.mapsworldwide.co.uk
McPhee	www.mcphee.com
Names UK	www.namesuk.com/store.html
Penshop	www.penshop.co.uk
Pixieland	www.pixieland.co.uk
Siam Presents	www.clickandbuild.com/cnb/shop/siam-presents
Silly Jokes	www.sillyjokes.co.uk
Silver Direct	www.silver-direct.co.uk
Star Registry — Name A Star!	www.starregistry.co.uk
UKool	www.ukool.com
Virtually Holland	www.vholland.com
WooduLike	www.wood-u-like.co.uk

gifts

health & beauty

Although prescriptions cannot yet be bought over the web in the UK, you will find make-up, skincare, vitamins, haircare and everything else cosmetic.

Changes Live   www.changeslive.com
Clean, stylish site with advice as well as an extensive range of products.

general
aromatherapy
contact lenses
hair
men's toiletries
nutrition & vitamins
perfume
skincare
soaps

general

Sites covering cosmetics, hair, skin and body.

All Cures	www.allcures.com
Aloe Vera	www.aloevera.co.uk
Auravita.com	www.auravita.com
Baldwin & Co	www.baldwins.co.uk
Beautique	www.beautique.co.uk
Beauty Business	www.beautybusiness.com
Beauty Merchant (US)	www.beautymerchant.com
Beauty For Women	www.beautyforwomen.co.uk
BeautySpy	www.beautyspy.com
BellaDonna	www.belladonna-uk.com
Best Of British	www.thebestofbritish.com/shop/cosmetics
BeU	www.beu.co.uk
Birmingham's Pharmacy & Perfumery	www.pharmacyperfumery.com
Bliss World (US)	www.blissworld.com
Body Herbals	www.body-herbals.com
Body Reform	www.bodyreform.co.uk
Boots	www.boots.co.uk
Changes Live	www.changeslive.com
Clearly Natural	www.clearlynatural.co.uk
Culpeper House	www.culpeper.co.uk
Direct Cosmetics Ltd	www.directcosmetics.com
Eve.com (US)	www.eve.com
The Garden Pharmacy	www.garden.co.uk
Gloss (US)	www.gloss.com
Green People	www.greenpeople.co.uk
Gulfat (US)	www.gulfat.com/onlineshopping.htm
Health 4 Us	www.health4us.co.uk
Herbalife	www.lookandfeelgood.co.uk
ibeauty (US)	www.ibeauty.com
Island Trading	www.island-trading.com
Look Fantastic	www.lookfantastic.com
Lush	www.lush.co.uk
Magic Makeup	www.magicmakeup.co.uk
Molton Brown	www.moltonbrown.com
Passepartout Skincare (US)	www.fitandfirm.com
She's First	www.shesfirst.com
Smiles Unlimited — Dental Products	www.smilesunlimited.co.uk
Tea Tree Products	www.teatree.co.uk
Think Natural	www.thinknatural.com
Vitago	www.vitago.co.uk

aromatherapy

Active Aromatherapy	www.activearomatherapy.co.uk
Alexander Essentials	www.alexander-essentials.co.uk
Aroma Direct	www.aromagift.com
Celestial Designs Aromatherapy	ws.safestreet.co.uk/aroma-shop
Denise Brown Aromatherapy	www.denisebrown.co.uk
Fleur	www.fleur.co.uk
Gold Pure Essential Oils	www.aromatherapygold.com

contact lenses

The Contact Lens Store (US)	www.contactlenstore.com
Contact Lens	www.contact-lens.co.uk
Club Optique	www.cluboptique.com
Iris Online Contact Centre	www.iris-online.co.uk
One Stop Contacts (Canada)	www.1stopcontacts.com
Post Optics	www.postoptics.co.uk
Simply Lenses	www.contact-lens.co.uk
Spectacles	www.spectacles.gb.com

hair

The Hair Shop	www.thehairshop.co.uk
Hairtec	www.hairtec.com
Wigs By Dramatic Differences	www.dramatic-differences.co.uk

men's toiletries

Boat Race	www.boat-race.com
Gentleman's Shop	www.gentlemans-shop.co.uk
Grooming 4 Men	www.grooming4men.com
Manpak	www.manpak.com
MenLab	www.menlab.co.uk
Shave	www.shave.com

nutrition & vitamins

Academy Health	www.academyhealth.com
Health Foodstore	www.healthfoodstore.co.uk
Health Shop	www.thehealthshop.com
LA Muscle	www.lamuscle.com
Natural Bodycare	www.natural-bodycare.co.uk
Nutravida	www.nutravida.com
Nutrition Direct	www.nutritiondirect.co.uk
Vitamin Shoppe	www.vitaminshoppe.com

perfume

Fragrance Bay	www.fragrancebay.com
Fragrance Net (US)	www.fragrancenet.com
The Fragrance Store	www.fragrance-shop.co.uk
Interscent	www.interscent.co.uk

Norfolk Lavender

www.englishhall.com/nl/nl/
nlhome.html

OVS Net
www.ovs.net/acatalog

Perfuma
www.perfuma.com

Perfumania (US)
www.perfumania.com

Perfume Garden
www.perfume-world.co.uk

Scent Packing
www.scentpacking.com

skincare

Dermatique
www.dermatique.co.uk

Escential Botanicals
www.escential.com

Martha Hill Skincare
www.marthahill.com

My Skincare
www.myskincare.co.uk

Oriflame Swedish Natural Skincare
www.oriflame-cosmetics.co.uk

Skinlogic
www.skinlogic.com

soaps

Bano
www.bano.co.uk

Flowery Mead Handmade Soap
www.flowerymead.co.uk

Soap By Post
www.soapbypost.co.uk

Soothing Sensations
www.soothingsensations.com

hobbies

In this chapter you'll find sites for arts and crafts, needlework and several other time-munching activities.

Kiteshop   www.kiteshop.co.uk
Colourful, clear site with every type of kite imaginable.

general

Craft Supplies Ltd	www.craft-supplies.co.uk
Hobbicraft	www.hobbicraft.co.uk
Hobbies Plus	www.hobbies-plus.co.uk
Hobby UK	www.hobby.uk.com
On Tracks Model & Hobby Superstore	www.ontracks.co.uk
Toolman Fine Hand Tools	www.toolman.co.uk

art suppliers

Art & Photo Supplies (Italy)	art-store.3000.it
Art Worker Supplies	www.artworker.co.uk
Cass Arts Supplies	www.cass-arts.co.uk
Eliza Gallery Art Materials (Australia)	www.artmaterials.com.au
Frame Us	secure.venus.co.uk/frameus
Heaton Cooper	www.heatoncooper.co.uk

astronomy

Astronomy.uk	www.astronomy.uk.com

kite flying

Kiteshop	www.kiteshop.co.uk

metal detectors

Wittering Metal Detectors	www.witdet.co.uk

models

Hannants Plastic Model Kits	www.hannants.co.uk
Punctilio Model Kits	www.modelspot.com

needlework

Albany Hill Needlework Designs	www.albanyhill.com
Barnyarns Thread	www.barnyarns.com
Bredon's Sewing & Knitting Machines	www.bredons.co.uk
Classic Stitch	www.classic-stitch.com
Cross Stitch By Design	www.cross-stitch-by-design.com
DP Software For Quilters & Stitchers	www.dpsoftware.co.uk
Empress Mills Online Thread Store	www.empressmills.co.uk
House Of Patchwork	www.houseofpatchwork.co.uk
Sew & So	www.sewandso.co.uk
Willow Fabrics	www.willowfabrics.com

scrapbooks
Say Cheese Scrapbooking (US)   www.saycheese.net

stamps
Robin Hood Stamp Company   www.robinhood-stamp.co.uk

hobbies

homes & gardens

Everything you could possibly want for your home is
available on the web. The same goes for your garden,
whether you're looking for seeds or trees.

Maelstrom   www.maelstrom.co.uk
Slick site with designer-style accessories for the home
at reasonable prices.

Dig It   www.dig-it.co.uk
Excellent gardening site selling tools, ponds, furniture
and barbecues, as well as a wide range of plants and
trees.

homes
gardens

★ Don't forget *Department Stores* and *Electronics*.

homes
general
Including furniture and accessories for bathrooms and kitchens.

Arts Saisons (France)	www.arts-saisons.com
Bed, Bath & Home	www.bedbathandhome.co.uk
Cosmopolitan Home (US)	www.cosmopolitanhome.com
Easibuy	www.easibuy.com/shop/ powerstore.cgi
Easy Life	www.easylifeonline.com
EtcEtEra	www.innovativegifts.co.uk
JML Direct	www.jmldirect.co.uk
Living (US)	www.living.com
Maelstrom	www.maelstrom.co.uk
McCord	www.mccord.uk.com
Net Sale	www.netsale.co.uk/house-sale.asp
Nigel Hoskin	www.nigelhoskin.co.uk
Primrose Gifts (US)	www.primrosegifts.com
Raspberry Village	www.raspberryvillage.co.uk
Sala Design	www.sala.uk.com
Shoppers Empire	www.shoppersempire.com
Web Blinds	web-blinds.com

bathroom
Bathroom Express	www.bathroomexpress.co.uk
Lavabo	www.lavabo.co.uk
River Accessories	www.riveraccessories.com
Showerail	www.showerail.co.uk

diy
B&Q	www.diy.com
Boys Stuff — For Tools	www.boysstuff.co.uk
Calder Trade Supplies	www.caldertrade.co.uk
Cookson's Power Tools	www.cooksons.com
Direct Tool Sales	www.directtoolsales.co.uk
DIY Ltd	www.diy.ltd.uk
DIY Tools	diytools.com
Dwight Gray Tools (US)	www.tooldealz.com
Express Tools	www.expresstools.co.uk
Global Power	www.globalpower.co.uk
Handy Tools	www.handytools.co.uk
In2DIY	www.in2diy.co.uk
Multitool Leatherman Specialists	www.inml.co.uk/multitool
Price Tool Sales	www.price-tools.co.uk
Quality Tooling	www.qualitytooling.co.uk
RS Online	rswww.com/index.html
Rye DIY Home Centre	www.ryediy.co.uk

Screwfix	www.screwfix.com
Sealants Express	www.sealants-express.co.uk
Terratruck Tools Direct	www.terratruck.co.uk
Toolfast DIY	www.toolfast.co.uk
Tools241	www.tools241.com
Tools Direct	www.protradedirect.com
Tools & Fixings Direct	www.toolfixdirect.co.uk
World's Largest Hardware Store (US)	www.newulm.doitbest.com

fireplaces

Fires Online	www.firesonline.com
Flames	flames.estreet.co.uk

foundry

Tuscan Foundry Products	www.tuscan-build.com

furniture

Antique & Reproduction Furniture	www.antique-furniture.co.uk
Country Desks	www.countrydesks.co.uk
Furniturebusters	www.furniturebusters.com
Furnituremart	www.furnituremart.co.uk
Furniture Online	www.furniture-on-line.co.uk
Furniture Webstore	www.furniturewebstore.co.uk
Futons Direct	www.futons-direct.co.uk
House of Chesterfields	www.jf-upholstery.co.uk
Iron Bed Company	www.ironbed.co.uk
Jepara Indonesian Furniture	www.jepara.co.uk
Living Space	www.livingspace2000.com/uk
Medina Imports Moroccan Furniture (US)	www.medinaimports.com
MFI	www.mfi.co.uk
Ocean	www.oceancatalogue.com
Pine Online	www.pineonline.co.uk
Straad Direct	www.straad.co.uk

homeware

Buy Buzz (US)	www.buybuzz.com
Chiasmus	www.chiasmus.co.uk
Clickdeco	www.clickdeco.com
Contemporary Living	www.contemporaryliving.com
Coopers Of Stortford	www.coopersofstortford.co.uk
Craft Design	www.craftdesign-london.com
Ethos	www.ethosuk.com
E-Vivo	www.e-vivo.com
Home Elements	www.homeelements.co.uk
Hometonic	www.hometonic.com
Inhabit	www.inhabit.co.uk
Kennia Int'l Housewares (Canada)	www.kennia.com
Lady Daphne	www.ladydaphne.com

Marks & Spencer	www.marksandspencer.com
Mufti	www.mufti.co.uk
Mustavit	www.mustavit.com
Nubold	www.nubold.com
Pupsnuts	www.pupsnuts.com
Royal Doulton Cutlery	www.royal-doulton-cutlery.co.uk
Sue Clark Ceramics	www.sueclarkceramics.co.uk
Viva Home	www.vivahome.com
World Of Treasures	www.worldoftreasures.com

interior decorating

Farrow & Ball	www.farrow-ball.co.uk
Good As It Looks	www.goodasitlooks.com
Interior Internet	www.interiorinternet.com
Wallpaper	www.wallpaperonline.co.uk

kitchens

Dining & Kitchen	www.diningandkitchen.co.uk
Kitchen & Home (US)	www.kitchenandhome.com
The Kitchen Collection	www.kitchencollection.com
Price Right	www.priceright.co.uk

cookware

Claire Kitcher Work Surfaces	www.ckart.co.uk/tuftop
Cook's Nook	www.cooksnook.com
Gourmet Cookware	www.gourmetcook.co.uk
Hampshire Cookware	www.chefs-toolshop.co.uk
Kitchenware	www.kitchenware.co.uk
Lakeland Accessories	www.lakeland.co.uk
Lynda's Cookery (US)	lyndascookery.com
Metrokitchen (US)	www.metrokitchen.com
Pots & Pans	www.pots-and-pans.co.uk

kitchen appliances

1st Call Appliance Direct	www.kitchen-appliance.co.uk
2001 Appliances	catalogue.barclaycard.co.uk/ cgi-bin/d2001.storefront
Appliance Online	www.applianceonline.co.uk
Cookers Online	www.cookersonline.com
Freenet Electrical Appliances	www.freenet.ltd.uk
Home Electrical Direct	www.hed.co.uk
Household Appliances Direct	www.householdappliancesdirect.co.uk
Net Appliance	www.netappliance.co.uk
Trade Appliances	www.trade-appliances.co.uk
UK Appliance	www.ukappliance.co.uk
White Box	www.whitebox.co.uk
Woodall's Electrical	www.we-sell-it.co.uk/elec.html

lights

| Amazing Lightbulb Company | www.amazinglightbulb.com |

homes & gardens

linen

Giving Tree Online Fine Linens (US)	www.givingtreeonline.com
Linen Store	www.homelinens.co.uk

locks

Barnet Lock Centre	www.lockcentre.co.uk
Safety Zone Safety Solutions	www.safety-zone.co.uk
Walters Group	www.thewaltersgroup.co.uk

plumbing

Plumb World	www.plumbworld.co.uk

rugs

Mythology Rugs From Greece	www.mythology-rugs.com
A World Of Rugs	www.rugs-r-us.co.uk

towels

Towels	www.towels.co.uk

windows

Homestore	www.homestore.co.uk
Leading Windows	www.leadingwindows.co.uk

gardens
general

Birstall	www.birstall.co.uk
Dig It	www.dig-it.co.uk
e-Garden	www.e-garden.co.uk
Garden Supply	www.gardensupply.co.uk
Greenfingers	www.greenfingers.com
Online Gardening	www.online-gardening.com
The World's Garden	www.worldsgarden.com

barbecues

BBQ Shop	www.bbqshop.co.uk
English Charcoal	www.englishcharcoal.co.uk

garden furniture

Croft Studios Decorative Garden Features	www.croftstudios.co.uk
Goodwood Garden Furniture	www.goodwoodfurniture.co.uk
Easy Gardening	www.gardeners-world.com
Parkland Garden Furniture	www.furniture-for-gardens.co.uk
Trip Trap	www.triptrap.co.uk

machinery & tools

CMS Garden Tools	www.cmsgardens.co.uk
First Tunnels	www.firsttunnels.co.uk
Garden Buildings	www.gardenbuildingsdirect.co.uk
Garden Machinery	www.gardenmachinery.com
Garden Wise	www.gardenwise.co.uk
Mow Direct	www.mowdirect.co.uk
Mowers Online	www.mowers-online.co.uk
Pelco Garden	www.pelcogarden.com
The Ultimate Garden Hat	www.gardenhats.co.uk
We Sell It Outside Heaters	www.fiesta-heaters.com

plants

Bluebell Nursery & Arboretum	www.bluebellnursery.com
Capital Garden Centres	www.capital-gardens.co.uk
Crocus	www.crocus.co.uk
Dobie's	www.dobies.co.uk
Nicky's Seeds	www.nickys-nursery.co.uk
Palm Tree Centre	www.palmcentre.co.uk
Silk Plant Company — Artificial Plants	www.silkplant.co.uk
Woolman's Plants	www.woolman.co.uk

Abooga	www.abooga.com
Approved Diamonds	www.approveddiamonds.com
Celtic Watches	www.celtic-watches.com
City Clocks	www.cityclocks.co.uk
Direct Watch Company Ltd	www.directwatch.com
Ermani Bulatti	gotogifts.co.uk/for/bronze
eTreasures	www.e-treasures.co.uk
Fashion Crazy	www.fashioncrazy.net
Finecraft Jewellery	www.finecraftjewellery.com
Fortunoff	www.fortunoff.com
Gold Jewellery Online	www.gold-jewelry.co.uk
Goldscene Jewellery	www.goldscene.co.uk
Great British Jewels	www.gbj.co.uk
Half Price Jewellers	www.hpj.co.uk
Ice Cool	www.icecool.co.uk
Internet Jewellery & Gemstones	www.ijag.com
Jewellers' Net	www.jewellers.net
Jewellery Unlimited	www.jewelleryunlimited.com
Jewels	www.jewels.co.uk
Pearl-e	www.pearl-e.co.uk
Silver Plus Gold	www.silverplusgold.co.uk
Scottish Jewellery	www.scottish-jewellery.co.uk
Studio Jupiter	www.studio-jupiter.com
Sovereign Diamonds	www.sovereigndiamonds.com
Traser Watches	www.traser-uk.com
Watch Factory (US)	www.watchfactory.com
Watch Heaven	www.watch-heaven.com

lingerie

Check the returns policy of lingerie sites carefully in
case the bra you buy doesn't fit and you need to send
it back.

Victoria's Secret (US)   www.victoriassecret.com
A large selection of unashamedly sexy and flattering
underwear from this US giant is available online. Fast
downloader.

ladies'
men's

ladies'

Absolutely Me	www.absolutelyme.com
Agent Provocateur	www.agentprovocateur.com
Alchemy Lingerie	www.alchemylingerie.co.uk/main.html
Amazing Undies	www.amazingundies.co.uk
Ample Bosom	www.amplebosom.com
Beeva Garments	www.beeva.co.uk
Bella Lingerie	www.lingerieuk.co.uk
Billet Doux	www.billetdoux.co.uk
Bird Of Paradise	www.lingerieworld.co.uk
Bras Direct	www.brasdirect.co.uk
Brief Look Lingerie	www.lingeriefavourites.com
Carlton Hosiery	www.carltonhosiery.co.uk
Clever Pants	www.cleverpants.com
Domaine Fashions	www.domaine.co.uk
Easyshop	www.easyshop.co.uk
Into Fashion	www.intofashion.com
Josh Lingerie	www.tapitlocal.com/josh2000/ joshhome.htm
The Lingerie Company	www.the-lingerie-company.co.uk
Lingerie Monthly	www.lingeriemonthly.com
Maple Drive Lingerie	www.mapledrive.com
Marks & Spencer	www.marksandspencer.com
Midnight Express	www.midnightexpress.co.uk
Nile Trading Ltd — Thermals	www.nile.co.uk/system/index.html
Rampage	www.store.yahoo.com/ rampagestore/intimates.html
Rigby & Peller	www.rigbyandpeller.com
Smart Bras	www.smartbras.com
Victoria's Secret (US)	www.victoriassecret.com
Wolford London Boutique	www.wolfordboutique-kenmode-kensington.co.uk
World of Lingerie	www.worldoflingerie.com/acatalog

men's

Billet Doux	www.billetdoux.co.uk/forhim.html
Brass Monkeys	www.brassmonkeys.co.uk
City Boxers	www.cityboxers.com
Kiniki	www.kiniki.com

lingerie

malls

malls

A US concept, malls serve as an umbrella under which many different stores can be accessed. They're a larger version of the department store – you can buy anything and everything on these sites. A good place to browse if you're not sure what you want to buy.

Shoppers World   www.shoppersworld.co.uk
Long lists and links to online shops serving various regions in the UK.

AAA Australia Shopping Mall (Australia)	www.aaaaustralia.com.au
AAA Shopping Mall	www.aaashoppingmall.bigsmart. com/live
aBargain	www.abargain.co.uk
Barclay Square	www.barclaysquare.co.uk
Big Bear's Mall	bigbear50nj.freeyellow.com
Big Save	www.bigsave.com
British Shop & Save	www.shopandsave.co.uk
Cindy's Cyber Mall (US)	cindyscybermall.homestead.com/ store1.html
Countdown Arcade	www.countdownarcade.com
eDirectory	www.edirectory.co.uk
Emerald Mall (US)	www.emeraldmall.com
English Channel	www.english-channel.com
English Village	www.englishvillage.co.uk
Fantasy Mall (US)	www.fantasymall.com
Freeserve Market Place	www.fsmarketplace.co.uk
Intermall (US)	www.1mall.com
iShop	www.ishop.co.uk
Italy Store (Italy)	www.italystore.com
Mall Internet (US)	www.mall-internet.com
Mall UK	www.mall-uk.net
Market Suite Mall (US)	www.marketsuite.com
NY Style (US)	www.nystyle.com
Online Shopping Plaza	onlineshoppingplaza.com
Qing Lung Shopping Centre — Chinese Goods	www.qinglung.co.uk
Scottish Mall	www.scottishmall.com
Shoppers Network	www.the-shoppers-network.com
Shoppers Universe	www.shoppersuniverse.com
Shoppers World	www.shoppersworld.co.uk
Shopping Emporium	www.shopping-emporium.co.uk
Shop UK	www.shop-uk.com
Sold Here	www.soldhere.co.uk
UK Shopping City	www.ukshops.co.uk
Virtual Highstreet	www.virtual-highstreet.co.uk
World Wide Shopping Mall	www.worldwideshoppingmall.co.uk
Web Shopping Zone (US)	webshoppingzone.com
Wild Welsh	www.wildwelsh.com
World of Shopping	www.worldofshopping.com
Worldwide Buy (Italy)	www.worldwidebuy.com
Zoom	www.zoom.co.uk

malls

miscellaneous

Looking for something weird? A slice of the moon? Or some fossils, perhaps? How about some fireworks? Look no further...

Billy Bob Teeth (US)   www.billybobteeth.com
For some truly awful dentures and bad teeth, this is your one-stop shop. Be warned, however, that shipping to the UK is a hefty $50 flat fee. So perhaps it's just one to browse...

general
christmas
domain names
parties

miscellaneous

general

Anything Left-Handed	www.anythingleft-handed.co.uk
Billy Bob Teeth (US)	www.billybobteeth.com
Cabaret Mechanical Theatre — Handmade Automata	www.cabaret.co.uk/shop/more/autogall.htm
Cruelty Free Shop	www.crueltyfreeshop.com
Despair (US)	www.despair.com
Elite Titles	www.elitetitles.co.uk
Feng Shui Shop	www.feng-shui-shop.co.uk
Moon Shop (US)	www.moonshop.com
Psycholaborations — Music Created For Your Lyrics	www.psycholaborations.com
Star Registry	www.starregistry.co.uk
Two Guys Fossils	www.twoguysfossils.com

christmas

Christmas Loft	www.christmasloft.com
Xmas.co.uk	www.xmas.co.uk

domain names

Domain Experts	www.domainexperts.co.uk
Domain Names Registry	www.domainnamesregistry.org.uk
Go 4 Domain	www.go4domain.com

parties

Charlie Crow	www.charliecrow.com
Exult	www.exult.co.uk
Party Domain	www.partydomain.co.uk

fireworks

Party Factory	www.partyfactory.co.uk

joke shops

Gag Works	www.gagworks.com
Just For Fun	www.justforfun.co.uk
Chicken Shop	www.chickenshop.co.uk

motorbikes & scooters

As with **Cars**, not as many sites close the deal on bikes as you would imagine. The web is good for research, however.

motorbikes

scooters

motorbikes

general

Bike Net	www.bikenet.com
Harley Davidson	www.harley-davidson-london.co.uk
Motorcycle City	www.motorcycle-city.co.uk

parts

Bike Trader	www.biketrader.co.uk
Mett Bikes	www.mettbikes.com
Side Kick	www.sidekick.co.uk

scooters

Board Silly	www.boardsilly.co.uk
Cannon BMW	www.cannon-bmw.co.uk

   Takes email enquiries.

Scooterzone   www.scooterzone.co.uk

The following sites are useful for research but you
cannot order and buy online.

Lambretta	www.lambretta.co.uk
Piaggio	www.piaggio.com

music, dvds, games & videos

Because many sites sell a combination or all of the above, we have included them all in one chapter.

Listening to music from the web on your computer is now possible thanks to the MP3 format. This is a downloadable file of a song or piece of music. Once you've downloaded the file, you can play it back in a special MP3 player. You can also listen to music in real time live over the Internet connection.

You can buy videos online and wait for delivery – the old-fashioned way – or watch a video directly on your computer through your browser. Try 'www.eurocinema.com'. If your computer can't deal with the downloads you want, a message will appear offering you the option to download the necessary files, usually Shockwave.

general
dvds & videos
games
music
videos

general

101CD	www.101cd.com
Amazon (France)	www.amazon.fr
Amazon	www.amazon.co.uk/pcvideogames
Audio Store	www.audiostore.co.uk
Audiostreet	www.audiostreet.infront.co.uk
Blockbuster	www.blockbuster.co.uk
Boxman	www.boxman.co.uk
CD Universe (US)	www.cduniverse.com
CD World (US)	www.cdworld.com
DVD Street	www.dvdstreet.infront.co.uk
DVD World	www.dvdworld.co.uk
Encore Direct	www.encoredirect.co.uk
Fusion Records	www.fusionrecords.co.uk
Games & Videos	www.gamesandvideos.com
Games Street	www.gamesstreet.co.uk
The Ginger Shop	www.gingershop.com
HMV	www.hmv.co.uk
Interactive Music & Video Shop	www.imvs.com
Jungle	www.jungle.com
Mad About Sci-Fi	www.madaboutscifi.com
Megastar	www.megastar.co.uk/megastall
Mello Yello	www.melloyello.co.uk
Music 365	www.music365.com
Music Box	www.cheapdiscs.co.uk
Music Video Games Centre	www.mvgc.co.uk
Net Megastore	www.net-megastore.co.uk
Newart Vision (US)	www.newartvision.com
NME	store.nme.com
Now Playing	www.nowplaying.co.uk
Play 247	www.play247.com
Power Play Direct	www.powerplaydirect.co.uk
Sci-Fi	www.sci-fi.co.uk
Shop DVD	www.shopdvd.co.uk
Software First	www.softwarefirst.com
Spacestore	www.spacestore.net
Tesco	www.tesco.com
Tower Records	www.towereurope.com
UK Music & Video Store	www.musicandvideo.co.uk
Video & CD Extravaganza	www.videoext.force9.co.uk
VIP	www.vip.com
Virgin Megastore (US)	www.virginmega.com
Waitrose	www.waitrose.com
WH Smith Online	videos.whsmithonline.co.uk
Woolworth's	www.woolworths.co.uk
The Zone	www.thezone.co.uk

dvds & videos

Absolute DVD	www.absolutedvd.co.uk

music, dvds, games & videos

Access DVD (US)	accessdvd.com
Admit One	www.admitone-dvd.com
Assured DVD	www.assured-dvd.com
Atom Films	www.atomfilms.com
Bargain Flix (US)	www.bargainflix.com
Benson's World of Home Entertainment	www.bensonsworld.co.uk
Black Star DVD	www.dvd-store.co.uk
Buy VCD DVD (US) — Japanese Films	www.buyvcddvd.com
Carlton Video	www.carltonvideo.co.uk
Choices Direct	www.choicesdirect.co.uk
Digital DVD Shop (Australia)	www.digitaldvdshop.com
DVD Depot	www.dvddepot.co.uk
DVDream	www.dvdream.com
DVD Empire (US)	www.dvdempire.com
DVD Net	www.dvdnet.co.uk
DVD Shop	www.dvd-shop.co.uk
DVD Source Shop	www.dvdsource.co.uk
DVD Tidal Waves (US)	www.dvdtidalwaves.com
DVD Warehouse	www.buy-dvd.com
eDVD Online	www.edvdonline.com
Film Store	www.filmstore.co.uk
Film World	www.filmworld.co.uk
Film Worldwide (US)	www.filmworldwide.com
Global Video	www.globalvideo.co.uk
Go DVD	www.godvd.co.uk
Goggle Eyes	www.goggle-eyes.com
iDVD	www.idvd.uk.com
Indian DVD Films	www.indiandvdfilms.com
Itchee (Hong Kong)	www.itchee.com
Ken Crane's DVDs (US)	www.kencranes.com
KVS	www.kvs.co.uk
McNo Ltd	www.mcno.com
Movie Mail	www.moviem.co.uk
Red Hot Monkey	www.redhotmonkey.com
Red Light Video	www.redlightvideo.co.uk
Region 1 DVD	www.region1dvd.co.uk
Sci-Fi Videos	www.scifivideos.co.uk
Send Me Movies (US)	www.sendmemovies.com
ThatzDVD	www.thatzdvd.com
Titan DVD	www.titandvd.co.uk
UK Disc Shop	www.uk.discshop.com
UK DVD	www.ukdvd.com
Video Biz (US)	www.vid-biz.com
Video Cave (US)	www.videocave.com
Video Ezy (Australia)	www.ezydvd.com.au
Video Shift (Australia)	www.videoshift.com
The Video Shop	www.videoshop.co.uk

games

★ Don't forget *Software* in *Computers*.

Football Coach	www.footballcoach.co.uk
Fusion Records	www.fusionrecords.co.uk
Gameplay	www.gameplay.com
Games & Videos	www.gamesandvideos.com
Games Paradise	www.gamesparadise.com
Game Retail	www.game-retail.co.uk
Games Terminal	www.gamesterminal.com
The Game Zone	www.thegamezone.co.uk
Lots In Store	www.lotsinstore.com
Mac Games	www.macgames.co.uk
Sky	www.sky.com/games
Software Express	www.softwareexpress.co.uk
Strategic Simulations Online	www.ssionline.com
UK Games	www.ukgames.com
Ultra Violet	www.ultra-violet.com
URWired	www.urwired.net
VGA Planets	www.vgaplanets.co.uk
Visions Online	www.visionsonline.co.uk
Wild Things	www.wild-things.co.uk

music

general

121 Music	www.121music.com
Abbey Records	www.abbeyrecords.com
Action Records	www.action-records.co.uk
BOL	www.uk.bol.com
Borrow Or Rob	shop.borroworrob.com
BURBS	www.burbs.co.uk
CD 999	www.cd999.com
CD Paradise	www.cdparadise.com
CD Selections	www.cdselections.com
CD Now (US)	www.cdnow.com
CD Wow!	www.cd-wow.com
CD Zone	www.cdzone.co.uk
Ceedee	www.ceedee.co.uk
Chart CDs Under A Tenner	www.chartcdsunderatenner.co.uk
Cheap Or What CDs	www.cow.co.uk
Council Of Nine — Ambient	www.cofn.co.uk
Da Music	www.damusic.com
Dance Latino	www.ecuador.co.uk
Discount Music Store	www.musicforsale.co.uk
DJ Direct	www.dance-dj-direct.com
Dot Music	www.dotmusic.com/shop
Dress Circle — Showbiz	www.dresscircle.co.uk

Earcandy Music	www.earcandy.co.uk
E-Dance	www.e-dance.co.uk
Global Groove Records	www.globalgroove.co.uk
Hamlyn Firth Music — Irish & Scottish Music	www.hfmusic.co.uk
Hey Day — Rock)	www.heyday-mo.com
Istikhara Music — World Music	www.istikhara.com
Jamdown Records — Ska	www.netline.co.uk/jamdown
Jewish Music	www.jewishmusic.com
Juno — Dance	www.juno.co.uk
Kantuta (New Zealand)	www.kantuta.co.nz
Kids' CDs & Tapes — Music For Children	www.kidscdsandtapes.com
Killerprice CDs	www.killerprice.co.uk
Magpie Direct Music — Original Recordings	www.magpiedirect.com
Magpie Records	www.magpierecords.co.uk
Ministry Of Sound	shop.ministryofsound.com
Moving Music	www.movingmusic.co.uk
Mr Bongo	www.mrbongo.com
Music Aid Charity CD Store	www.musicaid.org
Music For Sale	www.musicforsale.co.uk
Music In Scotland	www.musicinscotland.com
Music Mart (Australia)	www.s-central.com.au/musicmart
Music Stop	www.music-stop.co.uk
Mute	www.mute.co.uk
Muzic Depot (US)	www.muzicdepot.com
New World Music — New Age	www.newworldmusic.com
Nuclear Blast America (US)	www.nuclearblast-usa.com
Online Records	www.onlinerecords.co.uk
Opal Music — Indie	www.opalmusic.com
Papa Jazz Music (US)	www.papajazz.com
Past Perfect	www.pastperfect.com
Plantagenet Music — Military	www.plantagenetmusic.co.uk
Tidalwave Dance Music Online	www.tidalwavemusic.co.uk
Time Warp Records	www.tunes.co.uk/timewarp
Townsend Records	www.townsend-records.co.uk
Voiceprint	www.voiceprint.co.uk
Y2K Music	www.y2k-music.co.uk

classical

Classical Communications	www.thegiftofmusic.com
Crotchet	www.crotchet.co.uk
Lowri Records	ds.dial.pipex.com/silvius/system/index.html
Organ First	www.organ.co.uk
Seaford Music	www.seaford-music.co.uk

mp3 & downloads

★ Don't forget *MP3s* in *Computers*.

Amazon	www.amazon.com
Crunch	www.crunch.co.uk
D Music	www.DMusic.com
E music	www.Emusic.com
MP3.com	www.mp3.com
Music Maker	www.musicmaker.com
Muzic Depot (US)	www.muzicdepot.com
People Sound	www.peoplesound.com
Razor Cuts (US)	www.razorcuts.com

secondhand

| CMS Music | www.cmsmusic.co.uk |
| Second Sounds | www.secondsounds.com |

vinyl

The Beat Museum	www.thebeatmuseum.com
Felch Records — Dance Collectibles	www.felchrecords.com
Juke Box 45s	www.jukebox45s.co.uk
Purple Haze Records	www.purplehaze-records.com
Sweet Memories	www.vinylrecords.co.uk
Uptown Records	www.uptownrecords.com
Vinyl Tap Records	www.vinyltap.co.uk

videos

Albavision Scottish Videos	www.scotland-info.co.uk/albavision.htm
BBC Shop	www.bbcshop.com/bbc_shop
Bygone Video	www.bygonevideo.co.uk
Cheap Or What	www.cow.co.uk
Cinema Zone	store.cinemazone.com
Eurocinema	www.eurocinema.com
Network Video	www.networkvideos.co.uk
Sportspages	www.sportspages.co.uk
Video Net	www.videonet.co.uk
Video Zone	www.videozone.co.uk
Vintage Video	www.vintagevideo.co.uk

music, dvds, games & videos

musical instruments & sheet music

Buy guitars, drum kits, saxophones and every other musical instrument you can think of on the web.

ABC Music	www.abcmusic.co.uk
Boosey & Hawkes	www.boosey.com/musicshop
Chappell's	www.shopyell.co.uk/chappell
Donmack	www.donmack.com
Drum Central	www.drumcentral.com
Eric Lindsay Music	www.elmusic.co.uk
Foote's Music Store	www.footesmusic.com
Guitar Superstore	www.guitarsuperstore.com
Hobgoblin	www.hobgoblin.com
Jump Music	www.jumpmusic.com
Look Music	www.lookmusic.com
Macari's Musical Instruments	www.macaris.co.uk
Mill Hill Music Direct	www.millhillmusic.co.uk
Music Sales	www.musicsales.co.uk
Musician Shop	www.strathmore-ent.co.uk
Oxfam Fair Trade Co	www.oxfam.org.uk
Pie Dog	www.piedog.com
PSS Music Ltd	www.pssmusic.co.uk
Regent Guitars	www.regentguitars.co.uk
Saxophones	www.saxophones.co.uk
Sheet Music Direct	www.euro.sheetmusicdirect.com
Sounds Great Music	www.soundsgreatmusic.com

office supplies

office supplies

Equip your office with everything from furniture to laser printers. Don't forget the chapters **Computers** and **Electronics** (**General** section).

general

Sites selling furniture and electronics.

aBargain	www.abargain.com/uk
Ace Office Supplies	www.ace-office.co.uk
Action Computer Supplies	www2.action.com
Ashfields	www.ashfields.com
Canon	www.canon.co.uk
CHL Office Supplies	www.offserv.co.uk
Click & Deliver	www.clickanddeliver.com
Euroffice	www.euroffice.co.uk
Office Online	www.office-online.co.uk
OWA	www.owa.co.uk
RS Online	rswww.com/index.html
Staples	www.staples.co.uk
Stat Direct	www.statdirect.com
Stat Plus	www.statplus.co.uk
Tonic Computer Consumables	www.tonik.co.uk
Top Office	www.topoffice.co.uk
Viking Direct	www.viking-direct.co.uk

air conditioning units

The Air Conditioning Shop	www.freeshop.co.uk/front/ The_Air_Conditioning_Shop
Optimair	www.optimair.co.uk
Tuscan Air Flow	www.tuscanairflow.co.uk

ink & cartridges for printers

Aah-haa Inkjet Supplies	www.aah-haa.com
Ink & Stuff	www.inkandstuff.co.uk
The Ink Factory	www.theinkfactory.co.uk
Inkjet 4 U Office Supplies	www.inkjet4u.co.uk
Integrex	www.integrex.co.uk
Printer Supplies	www.printersupplies.co.uk

paper & stationery

Faxcessory	www.faxcessory.co.uk
Net Stationers	www.netstationers.co.uk
Paper Select	www.paperselect.co.uk
Stationery Store	www.stationerystore.co.uk

telephones & mobile phones

4 Phones	www.4phones.co.uk
AC Communications	www.accomms.com
Bargain Phones	bargain-phones.co.uk
Beyond 2000	www.beyond2000.uk.com
BT Shop	www.btshop.bt.com
Budget Phone	www.budgetphone.co.uk
Buy A Mobile Phone	www.buyamobilephone.co.uk

Carphone Warehouse	www.carphonewarehouse.com
Cellnet	www.cellnet.co.uk
Dial A Phone	www.dialaphone.co.uk
ETC Communications	www.etccomms.co.uk
Freedom Phones	www.freedomphones.co.uk
Free Mobile Phones	www.freemobilephones.net
Ifone	www.ifone.co.uk
JM Communications	www.jmcomms.net
Miah Telecom	www.miahtelecom.co.uk
Mobile Bargains Store	www.mobilebargains.com
Mobile Now	www.mobilenow.co.uk
Mobile Phone Network	www.mobilephone-net.com
Mobile Phones Online	www.talkcentre.co.uk
The Mobile Republic	www.themobilerepublic.com
MobileShop	www.mobileshop.com
Mobiles UK	www.mobilesuk.net
One2One	www.one2one.co.uk
One Shop For All	www.oneshopforall.com/uk/ mobilephone_shop.html
Orange	www.orange.net
Orange People	www.orangepeople.co.uk
Orange Phones	www.orange-phones.co.uk
The Pay As You Go Mobile Phone Store	payasyougo.bizland.com
Phone Shop	www.phoneshop.uk.com
Phone Factory	www.phonefactory.com
Phone Warehouse	www.phonewarehouse.co.uk
Small Talk Communications	www.prepays.co.uk
Storm Mobiles	www.storm-online.com/mobile
Student Mobiles	www.studentmobiles.com
Talking Shop	www.talkingshop.co.uk
Talk Mobiles	www.talkmobiles.co.uk
Telephones Online	www.telephones-online.co.uk
Tiger Mart	www.tigermart.co.uk
Time To Talk Communications	www.time2talk.co.uk
Totally Portable	www.totallyportable.com
UK Phone Shop	www.ukphoneshop.com
Vodafone Retail	www.vodafone-retail.co.uk

mobile accessories

Accessories 4 U	www.accessories4u.co.uk
Axex	www.axex.co.uk
Beyond 2000	www.beyond-2000.co.uk
Mobile Facias	www.mobilefacias.co.uk
Mobile Rings – Nokia Only	www.mobilerings.co.uk
Mobile Tones – Nokia Only	www.mobiletones.com
Ringtones	www.ringtones.co.uk

pets

We're not condoning the purchase of animals over the web – though rumour has it that this is entirely possible. But we do believe in getting someone else to deliver bulky cat litter and dog food supplies to the door. You can even buy aquariums.

Bouldercraft Pet Memorials   www.bouldercraft.com
For the truly pet-obsessed, remember your darling in style with a personalised gravestone.

general
birds
cats
dogs
fish
gifts for animal nuts
horses
medical

general

Animail	www.animail.co.uk
Bouldercraft Pet Memorials	www.bouldercraft.com
Champion Pets	www.championpets.co.uk
Farmrite Animal Health	www.farmrite.co.uk
Grannie's Pet Supermarket	www.granniespets.co.uk
Headstart Pets	www.headstartpets.co.uk
Noah's Cupboard	www.noahs-cupboard.co.uk
Over The Top — Products For Vehicles & Homes	www.overthetop.co.uk
Pet Emporium	www.petemporium.co.uk
Pet Market (US)	www.petmarket.com
Pet Planet	www.petplanet.co.uk
Pet Spark	www.petspark.com
Pet Store (US)	www.petstore.com
Pets Pyjamas	www.pets-pyjamas.co.uk
Petz	www.petz.co.uk
Whale & Dolphin Conservation Society	www.wdcs.org

Adopt a whale or dolphin.

birds

CJ Wild Bird Food	www.birdfood.co.uk

cats

Cat Fanatics	www.catfanatics.com
Cats' Protection League	www.cats.org.uk/shop.html

dogs

Barbara's Canine Catering (US)	www.k9treat.com
Puchie — Dog Collars	www.net800.co.uk/netstart/puchie
Sit Stay (US)	www.sitstay.com

fish

Aquatics Warehouse	www.aquatics-warehouse.co.uk
Edkin's Aquatics	www.edkins.com

gifts for animal nuts

Animal Crackers	www.k9gifts.com
Animal Designs (US)	www.animaldesigns.com
Catmandrew! — Cat Art... (US)	www.catmandrew.com
Cowtraders	gotogifts.co.uk/for/cows
Pet Bookshop	www.petbookshop.com
Pet Pro (US)	www.petpro.com
Top Dog Designs (US) — Dog Stuff For Dog People	www.topdogdesigns.com

horses

Equinat Natural Products For
  Horses   www.aromesse.com
RB Equestrian   www.rbe.co.uk
TDS Saddlers   www.tds-saddlers.com
Trailriders — Aussie Saddle
  Specialists   www.trailriders.co.uk

medical

PetMC — Pet Medical Centre   www.petmc.co.uk
Vet Medic   www.vet-medic.com

pets

shoes

men & women
men only

men & women

Barratt's	www.barratts.co.uk
Clifford James	www.clifford-james.co.uk
Jones Bootmaker	www.jonesbootmaker.com
Ozzy's Discount Footwear	www.ozzys.co.uk
Regalos Country & Western Store – Cowboy Boots	www.linedancing.co.uk
Safety Footwear Shop	www.idml.co.uk
Shopeeze	www.shopeeze.com
Softmoc (US)	www.softmoc.com
Shipton & Heneage	www.shiphen.com
Shoedini (US)	www.shoedini.com
Shoes Direct	www.shoesdirect.co.uk
Shoe Shop	shoe-shop.com
Sports Shoes	www.sportsshoes.co.uk

men only

Bexley (France)	www.bexley.com
Big Men Big Feet	www.largemen.co.uk
Big Shoes	www.bigshoes.com
Crockers Of Hungerford	www.classicshoes.co.uk
Ducker & Son	www.duckerandson.co.uk
Eastwood Clothing	www.eastwoodclothing.com
Marcus Shoes	www.marcusshoes.com
Pediwear	www.pediwear.co.uk
Tim Little	www.timlittle.com

sports

sports

The number of sports sites is vast – the football clubs
alone are numerous – whether you're looking for kit
to play in or equipment to play with.

Sporty Shop   www.sportyshop.co.uk
An excellent range of sports equipment and wear,
covering tennis, football, cricket, badminton and more.

clothing
equipment
souvenirs

clothing
general

Discount Sports	www.discountsports.co.uk
Footlocker (US)	www.footlocker.com
Porelle Drys Socks	www.porelledrys.com
Sneaker (US)	www.sneaker.com
Subside	www.subside.co.uk
Sports Mart	www.sportsmart.co.uk
Sportswearhouse	www.sportswearhouse.co.uk
Sportzwear	www.sportzwear.com
Surf On The Net	www.surfonthenet.co.uk
Sweatshop	www.sweatshop.co.uk

boarders

Headstrong	www.headstrong.co.uk

camping & outdoors

Carry On Clothing	www.carryonclothing.co.uk
Rohan	www.rohan.co.uk

football

The Arsenal Shop	www.arsenal.co.uk
Aston Villa FC	www.astonvilla-fc.co.uk
Birmingham City FC	www.bcfc.com
Charlton Athletic FC	www.charlton-athletic.co.uk
Chelsea FC	www.chelseafc.co.uk
Colborne Trophies	www.awards.org.uk
England Direct	www.england-direct.com
Fulham FC	www.fulhamfc.co.uk
Ipswich Town FC	www.itfcshop.co.uk
Leeds United FC	www.lufc.co.uk
Manchester City FC	ssl.mcfc.co.uk/mcfc
Manchester United FC	shop.manutd.com
Newcastle United FC	www.nufc.co.uk
Nottingham Forest FC	www.nottinghamforest.co.uk
Oxford United FC	www.oufc.co.uk
Rangers Online	www.rangers.co.uk
Sheffield Wednesday FC	www.swfc.co.uk
Soccer2000	www.soccer2000uk.com
Soccerbox	www.soccerbox.com

An index of all other football club shopping sites.

SoccerScene	www.soccerscene.com
Southampton FC	www.ssl.saintsfc.co.uk/sfcstore
Toffs	www.toffs.co.uk
Tottenham Hotspur FC	www.spurs.co.uk
Watford FC	www.watfordfc.com
West Bromwich Albion FC	www.wba.co.uk
West Ham United FC	www.whufc.co.uk
York City FC	www.yorkcityfc.co.uk

sports

riding

Caldene Riding Wear   www.caldene.co.uk

support

Proline Supports   www.proline-supports.co.uk

equipment
general

Adidas   www.eu.adidas.com/uk/thestore
All Sports Emporium (US)   www.aplace2shop.com
Dragon Sports   www.dragonsports.co.uk
Ealing Sports — Table Tennis,
  Tennis, Gym, Pool, Snooker &
  Croquet   www.ealingsports.co.uk
Kitbag — Rugby, Football & Cricket   www.kitbag.com
Newitt's   www.newitts.com
Outdoor Megastore   www.outdoormegastore.co.uk
Simply Sports   www.simplysports.co.uk
Sportackle   www.sportackle.com
Sport Authority (US)   www.thesportsauthority.com
Sportsking Online   www.sportsking.co.uk
Sporty Shop   www.sportyshop.co.uk
Stadium Intersport   www.stadium-intersport.com
Sweatband   www.sweatband.com
Total Sports   www.totalsportsconnection.com

angling

Angling UK   www.anglinguk.net
Basspro Shops (US)   www.basspro-shops.com
Dick Clegg's Internet Fishing Shop   www.internettackleshop.co.uk
Fishing Online   www.fishingonline.net
Fishing Warehouse   www.fishingwarehouse.co.uk
Fishtec   www.fishtec.co.uk/fishtec
Fly Mail   www.flymail.com
Harris Angling Co   www.harrisangling.co.uk
iShop   www.ishop.co.uk/cgi-
                                               bin/list_shops_new?6
Lakes Fly Fishing   www.lakesflyfishing.com
Nimpopo Online Fishing Tackle
  Shops   www.nimpopo.com
Sport Shop Online   www.sportshoponline.co.uk
Tackleshop   www.tackleshop.co.uk
Veal's Mail Order   www.veals-mail-order.co.uk
Walton & Skues   www.waltonskues.co.uk
Willy Worms   www.willyworms.co.uk
WP Adams   www.adamsfishing.co.uk
Yateley Angling Centre   www.yateleyanglingcentre.co.uk

sports

balls

All Balls	www.allballs.co.uk
Just Balls	www.justballs.com

camping & outdoors

9feet	www.9feet.com
Adventure Kit	www.adventurekit.co.uk
Black's	www.blacks.co.uk
The Complete Outdoors	www.complete-outdoors.co.uk
Downshire Caravans & Camping	www.downshirecaravans.com
England's	www.englands1.com
Explorers Online	www.explorers-online.com
Force 10	welcome.to/force10
The Gorge Outdoors	www.gorgeoutdoors.co.uk
Hike & Bike	www.hikeandbike.co.uk
Hugh Lewis Outdoors Leisure & Camping	www.outdoor-leisure.com
Oddball's Active Sports	www.fsmarketplace.co.uk/ oddballsactivesports
Oswald Bailey	www.outdoorgear.co.uk
Outdoor 2 Go	www.outdoor2go.co.uk
Outdoor Man	www.outdoorman.co.uk
Outdoor Supplies	www.outdoorsupplies.co.uk
Outdoor Trading	www.outdoortrading.com
Pedometers	www.pedometers.co.uk
Pyromid Outdoor Cooking Systems	www.pyromideuropeltd.com
Towsure	www.towsure.com
Wild Day	www.wildday.com

cricket

Cricketer Shop	www.cricketer.com/asp/ shop/shop.asp
Nottinghamshire County Cricket Club	bt.icat.com/store/nottscccsales

croquet

Jaques Croquet	www.smarte.net/croquet_online_ shop.htm

cycling

Avon Valley Cyclery	www.bikeshop.uk.com
Backyard BMX Shop	www.backyard-online.com
Bicycle Net Online	www.bicyclenet.co.uk
Bikepark	www.bikepark.co.uk
Buy Direct Bike Direct	www.bike-direct.co.uk
Cycle Store	www.cyclestore.co.uk
Cycle Stuff	www.cyclestuff.co.uk

sports

Cycle Tyres	www.cycletyres.co.uk
Cycle Xpress	www.cyclexpress.co.uk
Edinburgh Bicycle	www.edinburgh-bicycle.co.uk
Folding Bikes	www.foldingbikes.co.uk
Free Wheel	www.freewheel.co.uk
Geared Up Cycle Sports	www.users.globalnet.co.uk/~cycle
Hike & Bike	www.hikeandbike.co.uk
Launch Bikes	www.launchbikes.co.uk
Leisure Lakes Mountain Bikes	www.leisure-lakes.co.uk
Mountain Tamers	ws.safestreet.co.uk/mountain-tamers
Munrica	www.munrica.com
Pashley Cycles	www.pashley.co.uk
Settle Cycles	www.settlecycles.co.uk
Single Track Bikes	www.singletrack.co.uk
St John St Cycles	www.sjscycles.com
Ultimate Bikes	www.ultimatebikes.co.uk
Webcyclery	www.webcyclery.com
Wiggle	www.wiggle.co.uk

football

★ Don't forget *Clothing* in *Sports*.

Footwall (UK) Ltd	www.footwall.com
Ladies Football Directory	www.sunday-football.net

formula one

Ferrari Merchandise	www.ferrarimerchandise.com
Formula One World	www.formulaoneworld.co.uk

golf

Amazing Golf	www.amazinggolf.co.uk
Centre Golf	www.discountgolfstore.co.uk
Easy Golf	www.easygolf.co.uk
Golf 4 Less	www.golf4less.co.uk
Golfstore	www.golfstore.co.uk
Hip Action	www.hipaction.com
IT Golf Shop	www.itgolfshop.co.uk
Nevada Bob	www.nevadabob.co.uk
On Golf	www.ongolf.co.uk
Online Golf	www.onlinegolf.co.uk
Pellar Products	www.pellar.co.uk
Roger Williams Golf Shop	www.rcwgolf.co.uk
Shop Ecosse Golf Clothing	www.shopecosse.com
West Georgia Golf Co (US)	www.wgagolf.com

home exercise

Exercise Fitness & Leisure	www.exercise.co.uk
Gymworld	www.gymworld.co.uk
Petworth House	www.petworth-house.co.uk
TST Leisure	www.tstleisure.co.uk

martial arts

Martial Arts Catalogue   www.multishop.co.uk
Martial Art Superstore   www.martialartsuperstore.com

motorcross

Go-Moto   www.gomoto.co.uk

mountaineering

★ Don't forget *Camping & Outdoors* in *Sports.*

Ellis Brigham   www.ellis-brigham.com
Outside Now   www.outsidenow.co.uk
Rock & Run   www.rockrun.com
Snow & Rock   www.snowandrock.com
Urban Rock   www.urbanrock.com

paragliding

Airways   www.airways.uk.com
Sky Dragons   www.skydragons.com

riding

Cox The Saddler   www.saddler.co.uk
Frogpool Manor Saddlers   www.frogpool.com
Fox Saddlers   www.foxsaddlers.com
RB Equestrian   www.rbe.co.uk
Tack & Ski   www.tackandski.co.uk

rugby

Bristol Rugby Club   www.bristolrugby.co.uk
Canterbury Of New Zealand   www.canterbury.gb.com
Full Kit   www.fullkit.com
Kit Direct   www.smarte.net/
    rugby_online_shop.htm
Rugby Football Union   www.rfu.com
Rugby Plus   www.rugbyplus.com

sailing

Genus Marine   www.marineonline.co.uk
Sailing Gear   www.sailinggear.co.uk
Yacht People   www.yachtpeople.com

scuba diving

Mike's Waterfront Warehouse   www.divemikes.com
Online Scuba   www.onlinescuba.co.uk
Simply Scuba   www.simplyscuba.co.uk
Underwater Photography   www.underwaterphotography.com
Watertrader   www.watertrader.co.uk

sports

skating

Kate's Skates	www.kateskates.co.uk
Legends Boardriders	www.legendsboardriders.com
Skates Direct	www.skatesdirect.co.uk
Wavejammer (US)	www.wavejammer.com

skiing

Line Skiboards	www.lineski.co.uk
Snow & Rock	www.snowandrock.com
Sportsking Online	www.sportsking.co.uk
Tack & Ski	www.tackandski.co.uk
Wavejammer (US)	www.wavejammer.com

snowboarding

Action Sports Exchange (US)	www.fmz.com
Complete Snowboarder	www.complete-snowboarder.com
Legends Boardriders	www.legendsboardriders.com
Outside Now	www.outsidenow.co.uk

surfing

Legends Boardriders	www.legendsboardriders.com
Watertrader	www.watertrader.co.uk
Wavejammer (US)	www.wavejammer.com

windsurfing

Watertrader	www.watertrader.co.uk

souvenirs

Ray Taylor Football Souvenirs	www.footballsouvenirs.co.uk
The Sport Archive — Photos	www.thesportarchive.com
Sporting Prints	www.sportingprints.co.uk

general
mobile accessories

general

4 Phones	www.4phones.co.uk
AC Communications	www.accomms.com
Bargain Phones	bargain-phones.co.uk
Beyond 2000	www.beyond2000.uk.com
BT Shop	www.btshop.bt.com
Budget Phone	www.budgetphone.co.uk
Buy A Mobile Phone	www.buyamobilephone.co.uk
Carphone Warehouse	www.carphonewarehouse.com
Cellnet	www.cellnet.co.uk
Dial A Phone	www.dialaphone.co.uk
ETC Communications	www.etccomms.co.uk
Freedom Phones	www.freedomphones.co.uk
Free Mobile Phones	www.freemobilephones.net
Ifone	www.ifone.co.uk
JM Communications	www.jmcomms.net
Miah Telecom	www.miahtelecom.co.uk
Mobile Bargains Store	www.mobilebargains.com
Mobile Now	www.mobilenow.co.uk
Mobile Phone Network	www.mobilephone-net.com
Mobile Phones Online	www.talkcentre.co.uk
The Mobile Republic	www.themobilerepublic.com
Mobileshop	www.mobileshop.com
Mobiles UK	www.mobilesuk.net
One2One	www.one2one.co.uk
One Shop For All	www.oneshopforall.com/uk/ mobilephone_shop.html
Orange	www.orange.net
Orange People	www.orangepeople.co.uk
Orange Phones	www.orange-phones.co.uk
The Pay As You Go Mobile Phone Store	payasyougo.bizland.com
Phone Shop	www.phoneshop.uk.com
Phone Factory	www.phonefactory.com
Phone Warehouse	www.phonewarehouse.co.uk
Small Talk Communications	www.prepays.co.uk
Storm Mobiles	www.storm-online.com/mobile
Student Mobiles	www.studentmobiles.com
Talking Shop	www.talkingshop.co.uk
Talk Mobiles	www.talkmobiles.co.uk
Telephones Online	www.telephones-online.co.uk
Tiger Mart	www.tigermart.co.uk
Time To Talk Communications	www.time2talk.co.uk
Totally Portable	www.totallyportable.com
UK Phone Shop	www.ukphoneshop.com
Vodafone Retail	www.vodafone-retail.co.uk

mobile accessories

Accessories 4 U	www.accessories4u.co.uk
Axex	www.axex.co.uk
Beyond 2000	www.beyond-2000.co.uk
Mobile Facias	www.mobilefacias.co.uk
Mobile Rings — Nokia Only	www.mobilerings.co.uk
Mobile Tones — Nokia Only	www.mobiletones.com
Ringtones	www.ringtones.co.uk

tickets

Tickets for the theatre, sporting events and gigs will be sent to you by post or courier once you have ordered and paid for them online.

Jim Russell Racing Driver's School www.jimrussell.co.uk
Be a racing driver for a day.

general
cinema
concerts
corporate
gambling
music
restaurants
theatre

general

Including concerts, theatre, sport and special events.

Aloud	www.aloud.com
Ananova	www.ananova.com
First Call Ticket Shop	www.firstcalltickets.com
Last Minute	www.lastminute.com
Sheffield Arena	www.sheffield-arena.co.uk
Ticketlinks	www.ticketlinks.com
Ticketweb	www.ticketweb.co.uk
Ticketmaster	www.ticketmaster.co.uk
Virgin Net	www.virgin.net
The Way Ahead	www.tickets-online.co.uk
West End Theatre Booking	www.uktickets.co.uk
What's On When	www.whatsonwhen.com

cinema

Odeon	www.odeon.co.uk
Warner Village	www.warnervillage.co.uk

concerts

Concert Breaks	www.concertbreaks.com

corporate

Adventure Shop	www.adventureshop.co.uk
Grange Air Champagne Balloon Flights	www.hotairballoonflights.co.uk
Dome 2000	www.dome2000.co.uk
Formula One	www.formula1.com
Horizon Ballooning	www.horizonballooning.co.uk
Jim Russell Racing Driver's School	www.jimrussell.co.uk
Out Events	www.outevents.com

gambling

Eurobet	www.eurobet.co.uk
UK Betting	www.ukbetting.com

music

NME	www.nme.com
Royal Opera House	www.roh.org.uk

restaurants

Reserve a table online.

China House	www.chinahouse.co.uk

theatre

The Mayflower	www.the-mayflower.com
Theatre Direct	www.theatredirect.com
What's On Stage	www.whatsonstage.com

travel

travel

Another excellent use for the Internet is researching holidays, be they summer, winter or skiing. There are a vast number of travel agents on the net and substantial savings can be made. Although many of the airlines allow you to buy tickets from their websites, you'll find cheaper prices with the online bucket shops. Check out bargains carefully for special conditions and additional costs. Many of the sites provide useful information on your destination.

Last Minute   www.lastminute.com
A brilliant idea that has made its creators multi-millionaires. Although not a traditional travel shop, there are excellent prices to be had on flights and hotels all over the world.

general
accommodation
car hire
coaches
currency
ferries
flights
insurance
trains
specialists

general

A2B Travel	www.a2btravel.com
Amber Travel	www.ambertravel94.freeserve.co.uk
Airline Network	www.netflights.com
A World Of Travel	www.worldof.net/travel
Bales Worldwide	www.balesworldwide.com
Bargain Holidays	www.bargainholidays.com
Beachbeats	www.beachbeats.com
Booking Master	www.bookingmaster.com
Click A Holiday	www.clickaholiday.co.uk
Direct Holidays	www.direct-holidays.co.uk
EBookers	www.ebookers.com
Escape Routes	www.escaperoutes.com
Expedia	www.expedia.co.uk
Flightline	www.flightline.co.uk
Global Holidays	www.globalholidays.co.uk
Just Holidays	www.just.co.uk
Kuoni	www.kuoni.co.uk
Last Minute	www.lastminute.com
Leisure Planet	new.leisureplanet.com
Lunn Poly	www.lunn-poly.co.uk
Online Travel Club	www.onlinetravelclub.co.uk
Thomas Cook	www.thomascook.co.uk
Travelocity	www.travelocity.co.uk
Travel Select	www.travelselect.com
Travel Store	www.travelstore.com
Travlang	www.travlang.com
Unmissable	www.unmissable.com
UTravel	www.utravel.co.uk
Virgin Holidays	www.virginholidays.co.uk
Well Connected Travel (Australia)	www.wctravel.com.au
Where Will We Go?	www.wherewillwego.com
World Travel Direct	www.worldtraveldirect.com

travel

accommodation

The AA	www.theaa.co.uk/hotels/index.asp
Australian Internet Menu	www.themenu.com
B&B Net	www.uk-expo.com/bnb
British Holidays	www.british-holidays.co.uk
E-Bookings	www.e-bookings.co.uk
Giroscopio (Italy)	www.giroscopio.com/english
Gleneagles Hotel	www.gleneagles.com
Hotel Genie	www.hotelgenie.com
Hotel Discounts (US)	www.hoteldiscounts.com
The Hotel Shop	www.thehotelshop.com
Hotel World	www.hotelworld.com
Leisure Hunt	www.leisurehunt.com
London Accommodation – Web Hotels	www.web-hotels.com/wᵣ

London Hotels	www.hotel-england.com
London Net	www.londonnet.co.uk/ln/guide/
	resources/hotel-shop.html
Miss Marple (UK)	www.missmarple.co.uk
Not Hotels	www.nothotels.com
Powell's Cottage Holidays	www.powells.co.uk
Ruda Holiday Park (West Country)	www.ruda.co.uk
Stay Here UK	www.stayhereuk.co.uk

car hire

Budget Rent A Car	www.budgetrentacar.com
Easy Rent A Car	www.easyrentacar.com
Hertz	www.hertz.co.uk
Holiday Autos	www.holidayautos.co.uk
Holiday Cars Direct	www.holidaycars.co.uk
Platinum Chauffeur	www.platinumchauffeur.co.uk

coaches

| Eurolines | www.eurolines.co.uk |
| National Express | www.nationalexpress.co.uk |

currency

| Online FX | www.onlinefx.co.uk |

ferries

P&O	www.poportsmouth.com
Red Funnel	www.redfunnel.co.uk
Sea France	www.seafrance.com

flights

Air Canada	www.aircanada.ca
Air Travel Guide	www.airtravelguide.com
British Airways	www.british-airways.com
British Midland	www.iflybritishmidland.com
Buzz	www.buzzaway.com
Cheap Flights	www.cheapflights.com
Deckchair	www.deckchair.com
Dial A Flight	www.dial-a-flight.com
Easyjet	www.easyjet.co.uk
First Call Tickets	www.firstcalltickets.com
Go	www.go-fly.com
Icelandair	www.icelandair.co.uk
	www.klmuk.com
	www.lufthansa.com
	www.ryanair.com
	www.sas.se
	www.skydeals.co.uk

travel

hotels

Stratford Travel — To US, Caribbean, Australia & Canada	www.stratfordtravel.co.uk
Swiss Air	www.swissair.com
Take Flight	www.takeflight.co.uk
TelMe Global Traveller	www.telmeglobaltraveller.com
The Travel Bug	www.travel-bug.co.uk
TWA (US)	www.twa.com
United Airlines	www.ual.co.uk
Virgin Atlantic	www.fly.virgin.com

insurance

1st Insurance Shopper	www.insuranceshopper.co.uk
Alder Broker Group	www.abgltd.co.uk
Annual Insurance	www.annual-insurance.com
CGU Direct	www.cgu-direct.co.uk
Columbus Direct	www.columbusdirect.co.uk
Eagle Star Direct	www.eaglestardirect.co.uk
Screen Trade	www.screentrade.com
Ski Insurance	www.ski-insurance.co.uk
Travel Insurance	www.travelinsurance-sms.co.uk

trains

Euro Railways (US)	www.eurorailways.com
Eurostar	www.eurostar.co.uk
Rail Europe	www.raileurope.co.uk
Train Direct — For First Great Western	www.traindirect.co.uk
The Train Line	www.thetrainline.co.uk
Virgin Trains	www.virgintrains.co.uk

specialists

cyprus
| Cyprus Holidays | www.cyprusholidays.co.uk |

far east
| Lee's Travel | www.leestravel.com |

ireland
| 12Travel | www.12travel.co.uk |

new zealand
| New Zealand Travel House | www.nztravelhouse.com |

skiing
1ski	www.1ski.com
Complete Skier	www.complete-skier.com
IGLU	www.iglu.com
Ski In	www.skiin.com

travel

snowboarding
Board It www.board-it.com

us
Uncle Sam's www.unclesam.co.uk

index of advertisers